MW01121458

160201

The Real McCoy

THE REAL McCOY

Andrew Moodie

Playwrights Canada Press
Toronto • Canada

Playwrights Canada Press
The Canadian Drama Publisher
215 Spadina Ave., Suite 230, Toronto, Ontario CANADA M5T 2C7
416.703.0013   fax 416.408.3402
orders@playwrightscanada.com • www.playwrightscanada.com

Financial support provided by the taxpayers of Canada and Ontario through the Canada Council for the Arts and the Department of Canadian Heritage through the Book Publishing Industry Development Programme, and the Ontario Arts Council.

The Canada Council for the Arts
Le Conseil des Arts du Canada

ONTARIO ARTS COUNCIL
CONSEIL DES ARTS DE L'ONTARIO

Cover painting "Seat of Knowledge" by Joseph Holston.
Cover design: JLArt
Production Editor: MZK

Library and Archives Canada Cataloguing in Publication

Moodie, Andrew, 1967-
    The real McCoy / Andrew Moodie.

A play.
ISBN 0-88754-902-0

    1. McCoy, Elijah, 1844-1929--Drama. I. Title.

PS8576.O558R42 2006   C812'.54   C2006-903387-0

First edition: September 2006.
Printed and bound by Canadian Printco at Scarborough, Canada.

Table of Contents

Reason Not Justice

Black playwrights have long taken history as their topic, and with good reason. Until recently absent from history books and other media of representation, the deeds and contributions of peoples of the African diaspora demand recognition. Performing history on their own terms, and subverting stereotypical representations of Blackness, these plays do not simply fill in gaps, or bring unknown facts to light; rather, they reconfigure the stories that modern nations tell of themselves.

Andrew Moodie's *The Real McCoy* in its text, and in its vivid premiere staging at Factory Theatre, directed by the playwright, opening February 2, 2006, documents the achievements and contributions of Canadian-born Elijah McCoy, whose invention of a method for lubricating steam engines transformed railroads. His invention is likely the source of the saying "the real McCoy" because others' versions of McCoy's invention did not work as well, leading buyers to insist on the original. Moodie's staging of this piece of African-Canadian history goes well beyond simple documentation, however, for the play manages to accomplish representation of what African-American poet Elizabeth Alexander calls the "Black interior," disclosing what she defines as the "complex and often unexplored interiority beyond the face of the social self."(4-5)

Moodie's McCoy is, indeed, deeply an inventor, obsessed from childhood with the second law of thermodynamics. What the audience of the play experiences is a mind at work, intensely engaged in contemplating the mechanical forces of the universe, continually attempting to create meaning as well as material artifacts; a man who feels deeply but for whom all is subsumed by his drive to find solutions. Inefficiency disturbs him; his determination to maximize effort produces, in Moodie's representation, not only successive versions of the lubrication system, but also, among his 57 patents, his collapsible ironing board and lawn sprinkler—in addition to a worldview.

An aspect of Moodie's handling of McCoy's story that bothered at least one reviewer was the play's apparently mild politics concerning racism. I would argue, however, that Moodie's handling of this issue is particularly elegant and rich. The son of fugitive slaves who had come to Canada via the Underground Railroad, McCoy lived in a world where racism was virtually unchallenged. Canadian soil meant freedom for fugitives, but rarely social equality. In the play, discrimination is most obvious in Michigan, where McCoy spends his working life, but it is part of his Canadian context as well, as is implied by his father's wary response to the teacher, who suggests that Elijah should go to university. It is suggested again in Edinburgh, in the jokes played on him by fellow students, and in his mentor William Rankine's initial surprise at his obvious brilliance. That McCoy defies White expectations of Black intellectual capacity is never expounded, only gracefully intimated, the racism—and the sorrow it causes— rendered obscene by Elijah's grace and dignity. It is McCoy's stature that puts society to shame; this effect was most striking in Maurice Dean Wint's elegant performance in the premiere production. Nor is McCoy portrayed as exceptional despite his brilliance: his father's cultivation of the young Elijah's mind and spirit; his mother's grace; both of his wives' articulate nurture; the common sense, mechanical skill and loyalty of his uneducated friend and fellow worker, Don Bogie, all serve to elaborate a community's inner life. The appallingly racist context of their lives, then, is understood, but it is not the community's focus.

In McCoy's terms, "all the evils in this country, the hatred, and ignorance, bitterness and greed are inefficiencies that corrode the gears of our society"(page 80), by implication forms of entropy, ultimately producing chaos. Entropy—and the struggle against it— fascinates him: "All systems, left on their own, tend to become disordered, dispersed and corrupted," (page 10) he notes. The struggle against entropy is the struggle for life. Through the language of physics, then, McCoy appeals to reason, not to justice. Moodie's McCoy is not consumed with anger because, as his father tells him, "Anger closes your eyes. When you get angry you can't see. Keep your eyes open..." (page 13). He believes: "The world is a complete harmony... whose sweetest mysteries... intimate the possibility of a life without suffering, without fear. Where every problem has a solution and every... solution leads man closer and closer to... the true destiny that the creator of all things intended for us. It is our responsibility… our indemnity, to struggle to achieve our true potential. For good, for justice. A full and generous love of our fellow man is within our grasp. I can feel it." (pages 24 & 25)

Yet entropy overtakes him. We understand his entropy not only as natural, the devolution of all life in death, but also, and poignantly, as the result of his struggles against sorrow: the death of both of his wives, and his unborn child, yes, but palpably the terrible racist constrains on his ability to realize his full potential. Moodie's play creates a man of immense stature, but not larger than life, only larger than the society that oppressed him.

—Leslie Sanders
York University

Works Cited

Alexander, Elizabeth. *The Black Interior*: Essays. Saint Paul, MN: Graywolf Press, 2004.

Playwright's Notes

This is not the real Elijah McCoy. This is a fiction. I changed many facts about his life to create a drama. It's a common practice. It's been done for centuries. The problem with doing this to Elijah McCoy's life, however, is that because of his skin colour, there is much doubt and suspicion surrounding his achievements and the true impact on the world of his inventions. I have to admit I'm guilty of it myself. I first came across his life at an opening night party in Calgary for a Linda Griffiths' play I was acting in. A Calgarian came up to me and asked if I knew where the phrase "The Real McCoy" came from. I was stumped. Then this Calgarian proceeded to tell me about a Black Canadian inventor (already I'm skeptical) who invented a lubricating cup that became so popular that people ask for "The Real McCoy." I have to admit, it took a late night Google to begin to convince me that Elijah could even exist.

And so I was faced with a choice; remain slavishly verisimilitudinous, or try and communicate the essence of what the man signifies. I chose the latter. And I take full responsibility for that choice. There are those who will never believe that Elijah achieved what he did. There's nothing I can do about that. And if you are a student, looking for facts, I'm sorry, I'm a dramatist, not a historian.

The play is intended to be an allegory, or rather, a parable. The theme of which is our struggle with the fundamentally entropic nature of the universe.

To this end, one note is of great importance. His love of his mother is deep. He starts the play desperately reaching through the past for her. At the end of the play, mother and son MUST have some kind of deep emotional catharsis. If there are tears from either character all the better. The second note of importance is pace. There are perhaps two or three pauses in the whole play. That's it. There are no blackouts. The end of one scene is the beginning of another. Each line follows the other. At the same time, don't rush through the lines. Come in with your line on time, that's all. The text depends on it.

—AM

Elijah McCoy

As a child, Elijah showed great interest in the mechanical devices and tools used on his family's farm. His parents were able to save enough money to send Elijah to school in Edinburgh, Scotland to learn mechanical engineering from 1859 – 1860. After graduating he moved to Ypsilanti, Michigan. The management of the Michigan Central Railroad hired him as a train fireman/oilman. At the time, it was the only job they would give to a Negro. He had to stoke the boiler and lubricate the steam cylinders and sliding parts of the train. One of the problems of hot, high pressure steam is that it is murderously corrosive to most metals, and a thin film of lubrication is required to protect and seal the steam cylinders and pistons. In 1872 Elijah patented his first invention, a self-regulating lubricator that utilized the steam pressure in the cylinders to operate the valve.

Within ten years, his device was so successful that buyers of steam trains and steam engines used in mines and factories would ask if the lubrication systems were "The Real McCoy." But in post-Civil War America, few were willing to recognize that a Negro had developed the device. In 1928, he was admitted to Eliose Infirmary, an asylum for the sick, poor and mentally insane. He died a year later.

The Real McCoy premiered at the Factory Theatre, Toronto on February 2, 2006 with the following company:

Maurice Dean Wint	Actor #1
Kevin Hanchard	Actor #2
Ardon Bess	Actor #3
Zainab Musa	Actor #4
Marcia Johnson	Actor #5
Bruce Beaton	Actor #6
Matthew Deslippe	Actor #7
Andrew Moodie	Playwright/Director
Crystal Salverda	Stage Manager
Jen Contant	Apprentice Stage Manager
Julia Tribe	Costume Designer
Steve Lucas	Set and Lighting Designer
Gerrard Chrysostum Louis	Sound Designer
Courtenay Hindemit	Head of Wardrobe
Wendy Robbins	Set Assistant
Ruthann Drummond	Lighting Assistant
Allison Mondesier	Hair Consultant
Michael Hooper	Production Manager
Gordon Peck	Head Carpenter
Alec Harmer	Technician
A. Shay Hahn	Painter
Ed Gass-Donnelly	Graphic Design

Character List

Actor #1: . . . . .ELIJAH McCOY
Actor #2: . . . . .YOUNG ELIJAH McCOY
                                        RAILWAY WORKER
                                        DON BOGIE
Actor #3: . . . . .GEORGE McCOY
                                        REVEREND WALKER
                                        DR. TILLY
Actor #4: . . . . .MILDRED McCOY
                                        MISS CAROL
                                        HARRIET SCHMIDT
                                        SECRETARY
                                        MRS. ELENORA LLOYD
                                        ANNE ELIZABETH STEWART
                                        GERTRUDE KEITH
Actor #5: . . . . .MIDWIFE HILLARY
                                        NANNY HUBBARD
                                        MRS. DONALDBAIN
                                        SABRINA COHEN
                                        SISTER MATILDA
                                        MARY ELEANORA DELANEY
                                        NURSE CUGNOT
                                        NURSE WILMA
                                        NURSE BLODGETT
Actor #6: . . . . .DIGGER
                                        SMEATON
                                        WILLIAM RANKINE
                                        REMUS
                                        MR. WILBUR GABRIEL PARKS
                                        LONG ISLAND JOE
                                        MR. LESSING
                                        DR. RABB
Actor #7: . . . . .MR. MAXWELL
                                        ELROY
                                        KINCAID
                                        MR. GOLROKH
                                        ROMULUS
                                        MR. BURGESS
                                        BOSTON PETE
                                        DR. GRANT

Lights up. ELIJAH enters with an umbrella. He walks to the centre of the stage. He looks at a pocket watch, puts it away. He closes the umbrella, tosses his top hat offstage. Actor #6 catches it. ELIJAH then taps his umbrella on the stage. The other actors enter. GEORGE stage right, MR. MAXWELL stage left. Actor #6 holds a broom on an angle that is the head and neck of a horse, Actor #5 holds a mop parallel to the ground touching the broom, the strings of the mop are the tail of the horse, a blanket covers the mop and broom, that is the body of the horse. YOUNG ELIJAH stands in front of the horse "petting" it. Once actors #5 and #6 have set up the horse and all of the other actors are in place, ELIJAH taps the ground again. Lights change. Actors start.

MR. MAXWELL	**GEORGE McCOY**
…time and time again keep that mare the hell off my property and obviously you didn't think that it was important enough to…	…know damn well my property line extends all the way over to Klie's Beach and you know it! And don't you give me any of that…

ELIJAH McCOY
   She didn't look scared, she just looked like she was in pain.

MR. MAXWELL	**GEORGE McCOY**
…if she was that precious to you, why don't you call on your good friend Bishop Strachan. I'm sure he'll set you up with a…	…is coming out of your pocket, not mine! There is no way in hell I'm payin for… I beg your pardon!!! You listen here, if you've got a problem with…

MR. MAXWELL exits.

ELIJAH McCOY
   She had jumped the fence the night before. Went out looking for her next morning and by noon, we'd found her, limping, her leg broken, on Mr. Maxwell's property.

> *GEORGE pulls YOUNG ELIJAH away from the horse.*

GEORGE McCOY
See, the problem is, there ain't no way to make a splint for an animal that size, and…

YOUNG ELIJAH McCOY
That's not true…

ELIJAH McCOY
We never had any proof but we both suspected Mr. Maxwell.

GEORGE McCOY
And eventually she won't be able to eat for herself.

YOUNG ELIJAH McCOY
I can feed her.

GEORGE McCOY
Listen. That's very kind-hearted of you, but… and this is something you got to hear, and you ain't gonna like it when you hear it cause I hated it when I heard it. You see that sun up there?

YOUNG ELIJAH McCOY
Yeah.

GEORGE McCOY
That sun, it shines down on the ground, and it warms the earth and that makes the plants grow and that feeds the horse and that makes the horse do all kinds of stuff around here. Eventually Daisy here, she gets old, and she passes away, and that's a sad thing cause it makes us think one day we're gonna pass away too. But the thing is, when she passes away, Mr. Tanner gets her skin, so that he can make leather jackets and boots. Mrs. Beckett, she gets the hair, so that she can make brushes and wigs and such and… awww, now, listen, there ain't no reason to cry.

ELIJAH McCOY
My first introduction to the second law of Thermodynamics.

YOUNG ELIJAH McCOY
I can make a splint. I can do it, Daddy.

ELIJAH McCOY
>Entropy.

GEORGE McCOY
>Tell you what, you just go do that.

YOUNG ELIJAH McCOY
>Really?

GEORGE McCOY
>You just go ahead and do that.

YOUNG ELIJAH McCOY
>Okay, you stay right there, I'll be right back.

>>*YOUNG ELIJAH runs off.*

ELIJAH McCOY
>To me, it just seems like an inefficiency to take the life of an animal like that because of a bone that, given time, would heal.

>>*Actor #2 creates a loud bang by hitting a block of wood offstage. GEORGE takes the broom away from Actor #6. Actor #5 takes the mop offstage. Actor #6 takes the blanket.*

>Still seems inefficient. To this day. Now, I had no great love for the animal. It had… ah yes, before I continue, I suppose I should… ahehm. My mother. A former slave. Runaway.

>>*Actors #6 and #7 enter with blanket. They raise blanket above their heads.*

>Born Mildred Goins. May 9th 1822. Garrard County Kentucky.

>>*ELIJAH pulls away the blanket to reveal MILDRED McCOY, who has entered the stage from a trap.*

MILDRED McCOY
>One time, I seen a coloured gal tied to the rafters of a barn, and the master whipped her until blood ran down her neck and her back and made a large pool on the ground.

GEORGE hands her a newspaper. Actor #5 takes the blanket from ELIJAH and hangs it on the set with Actor #6.

ELIJAH McCOY

She would read the paper to Daddy, so that he would know what's going on in the world.

Actor #6 takes the umbrella from ELIJAH and walks offstage. Actor #5 walks offstage.

MILDRED McCOY

There was a dreadful fire in Hamburg.

GEORGE McCOY

That ain't right.

MILDRED McCOY

Awful steamboat explosion in America.

GEORGE McCOY

What's the world coming to.

MILDRED McCOY

A disastrous retreat in Kabul.

GEORGE McCOY

They shoulda called on me.

MILDRED and GEORGE kiss. ELIJAH takes the newspaper from MILDRED.

ELIJAH McCOY

She could make a poultice out of dock leaves and slippery elm. She could tell your future from a deck of regular playing cards.

She stands and walks with GEORGE arm in arm, as GEORGE pulls out a harmonica, plays an old southern slave song. ELIJAH reaches out to her as she walks away. He yearns to touch her, but he cannot. Actor #6 enters, takes the newspaper from ELIJAH and leaves the stage. MILDRED interrupts GEORGE's playing.

MILDRED McCOY
> On my way back from the lake, I saw the spirit of my uncle Will.

GEORGE McCOY
> Did he say anything?

MILDRED McCOY
> He pointed at my feet, then he pointed to the shore.

ELIJAH McCOY
> My father always used to tell me; on the day I was born, there was a fire in the sky.

> > *A sun is projected on the blanket that was hung by Actor #6 and Actor #5.*

GEORGE McCOY
> Would you look at that sunset. Mildred? Come out here.

> > *MILDRED is breathing shallow.*

ELIJAH McCOY
> There was a rhythm to the wind.

GEORGE McCOY
> Mildred! Oh, Lord. Oooo, Lord. The midwife, she ain't here honey.

MILDRED McCOY
> Hand me…

> > *She points at the handkerchief. GEORGE pulls it down, hands it to her. She wipes her brow.*

GEORGE McCOY
> Should I… I should stay, but I don't know how to… hello! Anybody out there!!!!

MILDRED McCOY
> Go, get her.

GEORGE McCOY
> I'll go get her.

MILDRED McCOY
> Go, get her.

ELIJAH McCOY
> The second law of thermodynamics.

> > *GEORGE returns with MIDWIFE HILLARY.*
> > *MILDRED is in labour. She moans.*

MIDWIFE HILLARY
> Oh my. Alright. Now, George, I'm gonna need you to do
> exactly as I say, you hear me?

GEORGE McCOY
> Oh, my Lord. There's been a bowel movement.

MIDWIFE HILLARY
> That's normal.

GEORGE McCOY
> What should I do?

MIDWIFE HILLARY
> Clean it up.

ELIJAH McCOY
> The premier law of all science.

GEORGE McCOY
> Should there be this much blood?

> > *MIDWIFE HILLARY lifts MILDRED's leg, puts her*
> > *hand under MILDRED's skirt.*

MIDWIFE HILLARY
> Can you feel where my finger is?

MILDRED McCOY
> Yes.

GEORGE McCOY
> There's a lot of blood.

MIDWIFE HILLARY
> Okay, I'm going to ask you to start pushing.

MILDRED McCOY
> It hurts.

MIDWIFE HILLARY
And I want you to push towards where you feel my finger.
Okay?

MILDRED McCOY
Okay.

MIDWIFE HILLARY
Start… now.

MILDRED McCOY
Eeeeaaaaagh.

MIDWIFE HILLARY
That was good, now do it again.

MILDRED McCOY
EEEEEEEEEEEAAAAAAAGH!!!!!

GEORGE McCOY
Why is there so much blood!

MIDWIFE HILLARY
I'm going to need you to grab all the blankets you have in
the house and then make a tea out of the herbs in the pouch
next to my right leg. George!

GEORGE McCOY
Yes.

MIDWIFE HILLARY
Do it now! Okay, Mildred, I want you to…

> *GEORGE runs, hands the pouch of herbs to ELIJAH. He
> then runs to the blanket, he takes it off the set and takes it
> to MILDRED.*

MILDRED McCOY
Haaaaaaaaaa!!!!!

MIDWIFE HILLARY
Don't push, not just yet!

MILDRED McCOY
I'M DYING!!!!!!!

MIDWIFE HILLARY
Wait, wait for it. Hold on.

MILDRED McCOY
Haaaaaaaaiiiiiiiii'm DYINGGGGGGGGGGGGGG!!!!!!!!!

MIDWIFE HILLARY
NOW! PUSH! NOW!!!! NOW!!!

> *MILDRED releases a blood curdling scream and writhes as if she'd been skewered by a hot poker. Then, suddenly, she dies. MIDWIFE HILLARY takes the blanket and bundles it to make a baby.*

GEORGE McCOY
What happened?

> *MIDWIFE HILLARY takes the baby offstage. Offstage, an actor plays a high note on a harmonica. Actor #6 takes a white bowl full of water and places it on the stage. MILDRED walks up to the bowl and places water on her face. Lights down on GEORGE, he leaves the stage.*

ELIJAH McCOY
All systems, left on their own, tend to become disordered, dispersed, and corrupted.

> *ELIJAH walks over to MILDRED as he says the next line. He wants to touch her but he can't. Harmonica fades out.*

Everything, whether living or not, wears out, deteriorates, decays, disintegrates, and is destroyed. Entropy.

> *MILDRED picks up the bowl and walks in front of ELIJAH, she looks at ELIJAH and leaves. Actors #5 and #6 hum the note played by the harmonica.*

The supreme metaphysical law of the entire universe!

> *Humming out. NANNY HUBBARD enters, knocks at the door as ELIJAH finishes his last line.*

GEORGE McCOY
Come on in.

NANNY HUBBARD
Thank you very much.

> *YOUNG ELIJAH enters putting together the last parts of a wooden puzzle.*

GEORGE McCOY
Again I have to say thank you, I really had no idea what I was going to…

NANNY HUBBARD
Please, don't say another word. I am just thankful Reverend Davis thought of me.

> *YOUNG ELIJAH walks up to his father with the finished wooden puzzle in his hands.*

GEORGE McCOY
Now, I don't expect you to keep things all too spotless or nothing. I work until four-thirty. Elijah, he gets home from school around three…

YOUNG ELIJAH McCOY
Here you go, Pa.

GEORGE McCOY
Now try this one.

> *He hands YOUNG ELIJAH another puzzle, more complicated than the first. YOUNG ELIJAH walks away, sits on the ground and works on it.*

NANNY HUBBARD
Would you like me to have him fed by the time you get home?

GEORGE McCOY
Just leave him alone with a couple of books is all. The three of us can dine together.

NANNY HUBBARD
Fine.

GEORGE McCOY
He's not a problem to deal with at all. Got his smarts from his mother.

YOUNG ELIJAH McCOY
This doesn't fit, Pa.

GEORGE McCOY
Keep workin.

NANNY HUBBARD
Are there any foods that you are not particularly partial to?

GEORGE McCOY
Pretty much anything's to my taste. I ain't too big on sweets, but I ain't against them neither.

NANNY HUBBARD
I assume no sweets for the child?

> *YOUNG ELIJAH starts smashing the wooden puzzle on the ground.*

GEORGE McCOY
Hey hey hey, now what's going on here?

YOUNG ELIJAH McCOY
Stupid thing doesn't fit.

GEORGE McCOY
Now, hold on hold on hold on. Stop! Look at me. Look at me. And listen to me. Every answer in the universe is right before your eyes. You just have to see it.

YOUNG ELIJAH McCOY
But it doesn't…

GEORGE McCOY
I remember when you were just a little baby boy. You were so new to the world, you didn't even know you were in the world. Bees buzzing in their hives, dogs chasing cats, roosters in the hen house, and you could barely recognize your own fist in front of your face. A little time goes by and you could see a little bit more and a little bit more. I was always here, I was always watching over you, looking out for you, and then one day you call me Daddy. You put things together.

YOUNG ELIJAH McCOY
But…

GEORGE McCOY
Anger closes your eyes. When you get angry, you can't see.
Keep your eyes open champ.

YOUNG ELIJAH starts working again.

GEORGE McCOY
Now we should talk about compensation.

NANNY HUBBARD
Oh, now I wouldn't dream of…

GEORGE McCOY
I know that you don't got no man around the house. You
have yard work you need doin', you got snow to plow, you
got a roof needs mendin', you call on me and no other. If
I can't do the job myself, I will pay for the man that can.

NANNY HUBBARD
Really, Mr. McCoy, that's not necessary.

YOUNG ELIJAH McCOY
Hey!

GEORGE McCOY
What?

YOUNG ELIJAH McCOY
There's a piece missing!

GEORGE pulls the piece out of his pocket.

GEORGE McCOY
Well done my boy, *(He kisses YOUNG ELIJAH's cheek.)* well
done. *(another kiss)*

YOUNG ELIJAH winces at the kiss. GEORGE exits.

ELIJAH McCOY
If my memory serves me correctly, the kitchen was over here.

YOUNG ELIJAH McCOY
Read me another story.

Actor #6 enters, hands ELIJAH a book.

ELIJAH McCOY
General room here, with a fire.

ELIJAH hands the book to NANNY HUBBARD.

NANNY HUBBARD
One more, and then off to bed.

YOUNG ELIJAH McCOY
Can I snuggle in.

NANNY HUBBARD
Well, I... I don't see why not.

YOUNG ELIJAH snuggles into NANNY HUBBARD.

ELIJAH McCOY
My room was separate from my father's. Originally it was
a storage room but it was fitted with a bed and a shelf for all
my books.

NANNY HUBBARD
Now, I have here a story I know you're going to love about
the courageous exploits of a young Charlemagne...

ELIJAH McCOY
I used to carve into it here, and here, little images of
nonsense things, just to make it mine.

YOUNG ELIJAH McCOY
I want to hear the olden days book.

NANNY HUBBARD
The olden days?

YOUNG ELIJAH McCOY
About all those astronomers in ancient times.

NANNY HUBBARD
That's not a book for a young boy like you.

YOUNG ELIJAH McCOY
That's the one I want to hear.

NANNY HUBBARD
> Right then. *Ancient Astronomers. Have you heard of the Alexandrian astronomer Era… Erato…*

YOUNG ELIJAH McCOY
> Eratosthenes.

NANNY HUBBARD
> Thank you. *Did you know that he measured the diameter of the earth more than 15 centuries ago?*

YOUNG ELIJAH McCOY
> Get to the part about how he did it.

NANNY HUBBARD
> Oh, uh, *He knew that shadows cast in Alexandria were different from the ones cast in…*

YOUNG ELIJAH McCOY
> Aswan.

NANNY HUBBARD
> Very good.

YOUNG ELIJAH McCOY
> And so, he…

NANNY HUBBARD
> Uh… *He took a measurement deep inside a well in Aswan, and another measurement of a shadow of an obelisk in Alexandria a year apart, and because he knew the distance between the two cities…*

YOUNG ELIJAH McCOY
> He could calculate the earth's diameter at 7,850 miles. And his estimate was only .5% incorrect!

NANNY HUBBARD
> Very good.

YOUNG ELIJAH McCOY
> He's a chump. I could do that measuring the shadow in the well out by old man Maxwell's sand pit and the church steeple.

NANNY HUBBARD
Well, you're not doing it tonight, cause now you have to fall asleep.

YOUNG ELIJAH McCOY
Nanny Hubbard…

NANNY HUBBARD
Yes.

YOUNG ELIJAH McCOY
You ain't got no kids, right?

NANNY HUBBARD
Why no. I… I don't.

YOUNG ELIJAH McCOY
I don't think that would be right. You being over here. They would be lonely for their mama.

NANNY HUBBARD
Yes they would.

YOUNG ELIJAH McCOY
Night.

NANNY HUBBARD
Good night Elijah.

NANNY HUBBARD exits.

ELIJAH McCOY
In the summertime, with it's effulgent skies of translucent blue…

Bell rings offstage.

GEORGE McCOY
Elijah!

GEORGE enters, he is shaving.

ELIJAH McCOY
…a pungent anarchy of earth and flowers would waft through the wood.

YOUNG ELIJAH wakes up and exits.

GEORGE McCOY

You get out of bed this minute, or you're gonna be late!

> *GEORGE exits.*

ELIJAH McCOY

But I have to tell you, there is something about the smart crack of that early autumn morning air.

> *Actors #5 and #6 enter. Actor #5 has a satchel that he puts behind his seat. YOUNG ELIJAH enters with his school project and puts it behind his seat. MISS CAROL enters.*

Something about how all the leaves are dying. Those pesky black flies are dying.

MISS CAROL

Children, quiet down please.

ELIJAH McCOY

As the world is muted, and the frost prepares the way for falling snow, one can finally focus one's attentions on the more serious aspects of this world.

MISS CAROL

Now, children, I left you with one assignment to accomplish, is there any reason why any of you couldn't finish?

CLASS

No, Miss Carol.

MISS CAROL

Good. Now, let's see what we have.

ELROY

I drew a mouse.

MISS CAROL

How is that an example of a device that helps mankind.

ELROY

He eats cheese.

MISS CAROL

That's good. Digger?

DIGGER
I did my report on the fire engine.

MISS CAROL
Very good. Elijah?

YOUNG ELIJAH McCOY
In ancient Greece, a man by the name of Hero created the first pneumatic device, which I have created here in replica.

MISS CAROL
Oh. Okay.

YOUNG ELIJAH McCOY
The sun's rays heat water in this closed tube. The sun's heat forces the water to decay in the form of steam. This creates a vacuum.

MISS CAROL
Yes, it…

YOUNG ELIJAH McCOY
This vacuum can be used to, for example, clear water from a flooded mine, like so.

He pulls at a string.

MISS CAROL
Elijah, that's incredible.

YOUNG ELIJAH McCOY
Oh. And… I brought you an apple.

YOUNG ELIJAH hands her an apple. Actors #4, #5 and #6 exit with YOUNG ELIJAH. NANNY HUBBARD enters with GEORGE and YOUNG ELIJAH.

GEORGE McCOY
Oh, it's too late for me.

NANNY HUBBARD
I could teach you.

GEORGE McCOY
I wouldn't dare put you through the struggle of trying to teach this old dog how to read.

She puts her hand on his shoulder.

NANNY HUBBARD
It would be my pleasure.

MISS CAROL enters, knocks at the door.

GEORGE McCOY
Well, I'll... I will think about it.

NANNY HUBBARD gets the door.

NANNY HUBBARD
May I help you?

MISS CAROL
Is there a Mr. McCoy here?

GEORGE McCOY
Can I help you?

MISS CAROL
I'm Miss Carol, Elijah's teacher?

GEORGE McCOY
Come on in. Come on in.

MISS CAROL
Thank you.

GEORGE McCOY
He didn't do anything wrong now, did he?

MISS CAROL
No, not at all. Elijah is a gifted, charming, very focused young man. And I would actually like to talk to you about that.

GEORGE McCOY
Sit. Please.

MISS CAROL
Well. Here's the thing. Our school is able to submit students to the head of admissions at the University of Edinburgh.

GEORGE McCOY
Okay.

MISS CAROL
And I believe, very strongly, that if your son keeps his grade average as high as it is, well…

GEORGE McCOY
My son at a university!

MISS CAROL
I can't promise anything…

GEORGE McCOY
You're sayin my son is going to a university?!

MISS CAROL
The one problem I foresee…

GEORGE McCOY
Uh oh.

MISS CAROL
The cost.

GEORGE McCOY
Yes. Yes of course.

MISS CAROL
Now I see no problem with a scholarship of $30 a year.

GEORGE McCOY
Oh, Lord.

MISS CAROL
No no. You don't pay that.

GEORGE McCOY
Oh. Okay.

MISS CAROL
But even with a scholarship, you're looking at $90 a year.

GEORGE McCOY
Right. Alright.

MISS CAROL
Now, I just received the application form. Think it over. I understand if the costs prove to be too prohibitive, but,

I really think that Elijah is a very special, special boy. And he deserves… well, I'm sure you agree he deserves the best.

GEORGE McCOY
Well, thank you very much. I'll definitely get back to you on this as soon as possible.

MISS CAROL
Nice meeting you.

NANNY HUBBARD
And you.

GEORGE McCOY
Elijah!

YOUNG ELIJAH McCOY
(offstage) Yeah.

GEORGE McCOY
Come in here, son.

> *YOUNG ELIJAH enters. ELIJAH hands YOUNG ELIJAH a book. YOUNG ELIJAH reads from it.*

YOUNG ELIJAH McCOY
Did you know that Leonardo Da Vinci… he made a steam gun, made of copper.

GEORGE McCOY
I didn't know that.

YOUNG ELIJAH McCOY
It's called an Architonnerre and you pour water on this part here that shoots steam through this tube that hits a bullet and boom!

GEORGE McCOY
(kiss) Well done my boy, *(kiss)* well done. *(kiss)*

> *ELIJAH hates being kissed.*

SMEATON/KINCAID
And did those feet, in ancient times…

> *ELIJAH hands YOUNG ELIJAH the satchel full of books and an assignment sheet.*

ELIJAH McCOY
I seem to recall walking down a hill to the foot of Edinburgh Castle...

SMEATON/KINCAID
...walk upon England's mountains green...

ELIJAH McCOY
There's a cemetery by an ancient church...

YOUNG ELIJAH McCOY
Excuse me...

ELIJAH McCOY
The grave of my namesake, my father's masters' forefathers.

SMEATON
Can I help you?

YOUNG ELIJAH McCOY
Yes, I'm looking for the Faculty of Engineering.

KINCAID
Classes don't start till tomorrow.

YOUNG ELIJAH McCOY
Yeah, well, I thought I'd get a head start.

SMEATON
How clever.

KINCAID
Well it's a good thing you found us.

SMEATON
The faculty has been moved.

YOUNG ELIJAH McCOY
Really?

KINCAID
That would have been embarrassing, wouldn't it. Imagine if you showed up here without your pigeon papers.

YOUNG ELIJAH McCOY
Pigeon papers?

SMEATON
You won't need this.

He takes ELIJAH's pieces of paper.

YOUNG ELIJAH McCOY
But that's the assignment sheet for…

KINCAID
Ten copies of the nine times table. Each on a separate page.

SMEATON
Pigeon papers.

YOUNG ELIJAH McCOY
I beg your pardon?

KINCAID
Well, that was my reaction.

SMEATON
Leslie Smeaton. Pleasure to meet you.

KINCAID
Jonathan Kincaid.

YOUNG ELIJAH McCOY
Elijah McCoy.

KINCAID
A McCoy. Fascinating.

YOUNG ELIJAH McCOY
So…

SMEATON
The new faculty?

YOUNG ELIJAH McCOY
Yes.

SMEATON
I'll draw you a map.

*SMEATON and KINCAID pull YOUNG ELIJAH away.
SMEATON hands him a piece of paper, SMEATON and
KINCAID exit.*

ELIJAH McCOY
There is a kind of walk that a young man has, when he gets it in his head that he is in tune with the whole entire world and not a single solitary thing is beyond his comprehension, beyond his grasp.

> *ELIJAH hands YOUNG ELIJAH a pencil. YOUNG ELIJAH writes a letter. As the letter is written, NANNY HUBBARD and GEORGE enter, they move across the stage, they grow closer and closer together. By the end, they are holding hands.*

YOUNG ELIJAH McCOY
Dear Father.

ELIJAH McCOY
The world…

NANNY HUBBARD
The world…

YOUNG ELIJAH McCOY
The world is a complete harmony…

NANNY HUBBARD
…who's sweetest mysteries…

ELIJAH McCOY
Mysteries.

NANNY HUBBARD
…intimate the possibility of a life without suffering, without fear.

YOUNG ELIJAH McCOY
Where every problem has a solution and every…

ELIJAH McCOY
…solution leads man closer and closer to…

NANNY HUBBARD
…the true destiny that the creator of all things intended for us.

YOUNG ELIJAH McCOY
It is our responsibility…

ELIJAH McCOY
...our indemnity...

NANNY HUBBARD
...to struggle to achieve our true potential.

YOUNG ELIJAH McCOY
For good, for justice.

NANNY HUBBARD
A full and generous love of our fellow man is within our grasp.

YOUNG ELIJAH McCOY
I can feel it.

ELIJAH McCOY
I can feel it.

> *NANNY HUBBARD kisses GEORGE on the cheek.*
> *YOUNG ELIJAH grabs his satchel and runs around*
> *town. Actor #4 enters.*

YOUNG ELIJAH McCOY
Excuse me, is this the Faculty of Engineering?

NURSE WILMA
Medicine.

YOUNG ELIJAH McCOY
I beg your pardon?

ELIJAH McCOY
There are three main founders of the modern science of
thermodynamics.

> *Actor #5 enters.*

YOUNG ELIJAH McCOY
Excuse me is this the Faculty of...

MRS. DONALDBAIN
Law? Yes it is, please, come in.

ELIJAH McCOY
Rudolf Julius Emanuel Clausius.

YOUNG ELIJAH McCOY
Excuse me, is…

HARRIET SCHMIDT
No dear.

ELIJAH McCOY
Lord William Thompson Kelvin.

YOUNG ELIJAH McCOY
Where did they move the Faculty of Engineering?!

SABRINA COHEN
Oh, dear.

> *Actor #6 enters. Stands behind ELIJAH.*

ELIJAH McCOY
And William John Macquorn Rankine.

WILLIAM RANKINE
God made man an imperfect thing. WE. DON'T. HAVE. THAT. LUXURY. Whatever we design must be perfect and true or else people die. God doesnee care if people die. We do.

> *YOUNG ELIJAH enters, trying to get to his seat, he drops his books on the floor.*

YOUNG ELIJAH McCOY
I'm sorry. I'm… I'll just…

> *He quickly picks up his books and hurries to his seat.*

WILLIAM RANKINE
You're late.

YOUNG ELIJAH McCOY
I am very sorry, I was under the mistaken impression…

WILLIAM RANKINE
No excuses. Sit down. If you're late again, you're out of my class.

YOUNG ELIJAH McCOY
It will not happen again.

WILLIAM RANKINE
We'll see about that. As I was saying. Entropy, second law of thermodynamics. The first?

YOUNG ELIJAH McCOY
Oh, me? The uh…

KINCAID
The energy within a closed system remains constant.

WILLIAM RANKINE
Very good. These two laws are the left hand and the right hand of God. And they are absolute. Learn them. You're going to spend the rest of your life in defiance of these two laws. With these hands, God pummels the earth. He takes away our loved ones. He shatters the lives of kings. He lays waste to the nameless poverty stricken masses cowering for a scrap of food left by dogs. Kincaid!

KINCAID
Yes sir.

WILLIAM RANKINE
Energy is related to…

KINCAID
Power over time.

WILLIAM RANKINE
Assignment sheet.

KINCAID
Sir.

WILLIAM RANKINE
McCoy.

YOUNG ELIJAH McCOY
Yes?

WILLIAM RANKINE
Where "m" is the mass and "v" is velocity, what is the formula for gravitational potential energy.

YOUNG ELIJAH McCOY
Sir, I have to tell you, a practical joke has been played on me, and I… I think you may find it amusing.

WILLIAM RANKINE
I am certain, I will not.

> *NANNY HUBBARD enters with GEORGE, reading a letter to him.*

NANNY HUBBARD
As you can imagine from the description, Haggis is not one of my favourite meals.

GEORGE McCOY
Sounds fine to me.

NANNY HUBBARD
I have however grown fond of a dish called Neeps and Tatties. I will tell you in my next letter what it consists of, so that for at least a few days you will imagine it to be more exotic than it actually is.

> *ELIJAH whispers into YOUNG ELIJAH's ear.*

GEORGE McCOY
How come he hasn't mentioned school yet?

NANNY HUBBARD
Mr. Rankine and I are getting along like a house on fire.

GEORGE McCOY
That's my boy.

NANNY HUBBARD
I learned from Nan Hubbard you had to sell part of the land to pay for my tuition.

GEORGE McCOY
Now, what the hell you go and do that for?

NANNY HUBBARD
Don't be mad at her, I just want to say your belief in me and support is greatly appreciated.

GEORGE McCOY
Now, it doesn't say that.

NANNY HUBBARD
If I could become half the man you are, I would be half the greatest man this world has ever seen.

GEORGE McCOY
All right. That's enough.

NANNY HUBBARD
Yours truly…

GEORGE McCOY
I know who wrote it.

NANNY HUBBARD
What's the matter.

GEORGE McCOY
That boy. That boy.

> *ELIJAH and Actor #5 bring on a chalk board with a chalk drawing of a steam engine.*

WILLIAM RANKINE
There cannot be a more beautiful and striking exemplification of the union of science and art than is exhibited in the steam engine.

ELIJAH McCOY
Mr. Rankine was offered by the Queen a position at Glasgow University where he would be working with some of the greatest minds of the time on some of the most challenging aspects of steam engine technology.

WILLIAM RANKINE
And I am offering an apprenticeship to anyone who solves this problem.

> *WILLIAM spins the chalk board. ELIJAH stops it to reveal the other side. It has the following question. "In a steam engine the condenser is kept at atmospheric pressure. How will increasing the pressure of the boiler change the thermal efficiency of the engine?" KINCAID and ELIJAH square off with pads of paper and pencils. WILLIAM pulls out a pistol.*

WILLIAM RANKINE
> Ready… set… oh crap how does this thing work. *(KINCAID tries to point out how it works. RANKINE pulls it away suddenly.)* Never mind. Ready, set, GO!

ELIJAH McCOY
> You can do it, relax.

YOUNG ELIJAH McCOY
> Okay, it was Papin who said air exerts pressure, so therefore a vacuum can do work.

ELIJAH McCOY
> No no, there are two kinds of entropy, remember?

YOUNG ELIJAH McCOY
> The conversion of heat into work…

ELIJAH McCOY
> …and the transfer of heat from high to low temperature.

YOUNG ELIJAH McCOY
> Why the hell is Kincaid looking over at me like that for.

ELIJAH McCOY
> Pay attention to the problem, not him.

YOUNG ELIJAH McCOY
> Now the value is too high. Thomas Newcomen made that mistake and Rankine knows it!

ELIJAH McCOY
> Relax.

YOUNG ELIJAH McCOY
> But…

ELIJAH McCOY
> The answer is there. You'll see it.

YOUNG ELIJAH McCOY
> But…

ELIJAH McCOY
> You will see it.

WILLIAM RANKINE
Time's up. Mr. McCoy!!!!

YOUNG ELIJAH McCOY
Done!

WILLIAM RANKINE
Mr. Kincaid?

KINCAID
Thermal efficiency is equal to atmospheric pressure over frictional loss times engine mass to the power of boiler volume minus piston volume.

WILLIAM RANKINE
Very clever.

KINCAID
Thank you.

WILLIAM RANKINE
And very wrong.

KINCAID
I beg your pardon sir?

WILLIAM RANKINE
McCoy?

KINCAID
But sir, I…

WILLIAM RANKINE
Are you still talking, Kincaid?

KINCAID
No sir.

WILLIAM RANKINE
McCoy?

YOUNG ELIJAH McCOY
Thermal efficiency is equal to one minus condenser temperature over boiler temperature.

WILLIAM RANKINE
And how did you come up with that.

YOUNG ELIJAH McCOY
Oh, it was a doozy sir. And I have to admit, I was about
to make all the same mistakes that were made before by
Newcomen, Papin and Evans. I was about to give up, when
suddenly I realized, for heaven sake, if the pressure of the
boiler is raised, the saturation temperature of steam will
increase and therefore the boiler temperature will increase.
That is, if you adhere to the theories of one Sadi Nicolas
Leonard Carnot, the man whose work you yourself have
been trying to substantiate over the past ten years.

WILLIAM RANKINE
Right. Well. Right.

>   *WILLIAM exits.*

KINCAID
Nicely played.

YOUNG ELIJAH McCOY
Thank you.

KINCAID
You are a worthy opponent deserving of my respect.

YOUNG ELIJAH McCOY
Yes I am.

KINCAID
There's an informal get together at Smeaton's family estate
tomorrow night. Would you like to attend.

YOUNG ELIJAH McCOY
Some other time.

KINCAID
You sure?

YOUNG ELIJAH McCOY
Yes I am.

>   *KINCAID exits. WILLIAM enters, drunk. As WILLIAM
>   sings, YOUNG ELIJAH tries to slink away, unnoticed.*

WILLIAM RANKINE
A PARTY OF ASTRONOMERS WENT MEASURING THE

EARTH AND FORTY MILLION METRES THEY TOOK TO
BE ITS GIRTH FIVE HUNDRED MILLION INCHES
THOUGH, GO THROUGH FROM POLE TO POLE, SO
LET'S STICK TO INCHES FEET AND YARDS AND THE
GOOD OLD THREE FOOT RULE!

WILLIAM sees YOUNG ELIJAH.

WILLIAM RANKINE
Pssssst! Boy! Come here!

> *ELIJAH walks over to WILLIAM. WILLIAM hands
> ELIJAH a Scotch and a cigar.*

YOUNG ELIJAH McCOY
Sir, I don't smoke.

WILLIAM RANKINE
Well you do now! God love you, you bastard, you gave it as
good as you got. And I'll tell you something, it is worth all
the gold in Persia to see the back end of that snooty upper
crust Kincaid, I'll tell you that. How's the Scotch?

YOUNG ELIJAH McCOY
Fine.

WILLIAM RANKINE
You and me. I'll make a master engineer of you, young
McCoy. Now, you tell me something.

YOUNG ELIJAH McCOY
Yes.

WILLIAM RANKINE
Tell me something.

YOUNG ELIJAH McCOY
Yeees.

> *WILLIAM looks around.*

WILLIAM RANKINE
I want you to listen to the question that I am about to ask
you and I want you to answer honestly, do you understand?

YOUNG ELIJAH McCOY
I understand.

WILLIAM RANKINE
Do you believe… that it is possible, to send a man to the moon?

YOUNG ELIJAH McCOY
I… wow. Uhm. I suppose… I…

WILLIAM RANKINE
Listen to me. It will happen. One day. I'm telling you. This universe… we are going to unlock the secrets of this universe. We are going to pry loose the hands of God, you and me.

YOUNG ELIJAH McCOY
Cheers.

> *To the heavens.*

WILLIAM RANKINE
You hear that you bastard! You son of a bitch! You have no idea what you have unleashed onto the cosmos! You son of a bitch.

> *A harmonica plays, made to sound like a train whistle, and then a train, moving faster and faster. GEORGE enters with NANNY HUBBARD looking for ELIJAH. As WILLIAM exits he bumps into GEORGE. Actors #4 and #7 enter and exit as people at the train station hurrying to their destination.*

NANNY HUBBARD
They said the trains were running on time.

YOUNG ELIJAH McCOY
Is that Old Man Tench's barn?

GEORGE McCOY
Now, you listen here, I don't want you pawing all over the boy.

NANNY HUBBARD
Oh, now…

YOUNG ELIJAH McCOY
I swear I don't remember Mrs. Beckett's filigree being green.

GEORGE McCOY
I'm serious, don't make strange. He's got enough on his mind.

YOUNG ELIJAH McCOY
Hey! Colchester's got a general store!

GEORGE McCOY
There he is!

YOUNG ELIJAH McCOY
Well would you look at that. I'm fading. I'm fading away.

GEORGE McCOY
Son. Over here.

> *GEORGE kisses ELIJAH on the cheek. YOUNG ELIJAH walks backwards offstage. Slowly.*

ELIJAH McCOY
Pop!

GEORGE McCOY
This boy, look at this boy!

ELIJAH McCOY
Let's get out of the cold, Pop.

> *GEORGE paws over ELIJAH. ELIJAH pushes him away.*

GEORGE McCOY
You have not been eating.

ELIJAH McCOY
How you doing, Nan?

NANNY HUBBARD
Better for the sight of you.

GEORGE McCOY
Now I want to hear all about how things went on your journey and all that, but first, I have something to tell you.

ELIJAH McCOY
Oh, yeah.

GEORGE McCOY
I got you a job.

ELIJAH McCOY
You did.

GEORGE McCOY
It's at the post office. It's just to get you on your feet, but if you wanted, I know for a fact they're gonna be needing a postmaster in these here parts and that's an office job for sure.

ELIJAH McCOY
Dad…

GEORGE McCOY
Sit yourself down. Nan's got a warm meal all ready for you.

NANNY HUBBARD
You still love corn bread, don't you?

ELIJAH McCOY
Listen, Dad. I got to tell you something.

GEORGE McCOY
What?

ELIJAH McCOY
I'm… I'm not staying here long. I should have told you. Mr. Rankine got me a job in Ypsilanti, Michigan…

GEORGE McCOY
Michigan…

ELIJAH McCOY
…working for a company that builds steam engines. I'm gonna get to do what I've been studying to do all these years. I appreciate you…

GEORGE McCOY
You're just telling me this now!

ELIJAH McCOY
I'm so sorry.

GEORGE McCOY
No no no. Please. Young man. My boy is making his way in the world.

ELIJAH McCOY
You can come live with me, Pop.

GEORGE McCOY
Well, we'll see about that.

ELIJAH McCOY
Mr. Rankine is the most amazing… he was like a fath… we worked on a process… it's kinda hard to explain, it makes steam engines more efficient.

GEORGE McCOY
It's alright, tell me about it.

ELIJAH McCOY
Well, steam engines, the smaller you make them, the more powerful and the more dangerous they become, and Mr. Rankine's always saying we must give the world perfection because people could die if we don't, cause the Lord has two hands, one of power, and one of entropy, and we have to fight the hand of God or else…

GEORGE slaps his son's face.

GEORGE McCOY
There is one perfect thing in this world and that is the will of God. No son of mine would ever deny that.

GEORGE walks away.

ELIJAH McCOY
Dad, I wasn't…

NANNY HUBBARD
Elijah. It's alright dear. It's alright.

NANNY HUBBARD follows GEORGE. Actors #4, #6, #7 and #3 enter singing "Chesapeake Bay," a railway

> *work chantey. ELIJAH tries to get Actor #4's attention.*
> *ELIJAH speaks over the railroad chantey.*

RAILWAY WORKER
Oh, Chesapeake Bay!

CHORUS
My lordy, ain't no money-makin country.

RAILWAY WORKER
Oh, Chesapeake Bay!

ELIJAH McCOY
Excuse me…

CHORUS
My lordy, ain't no money makin country.

RAILWAY WORKER
How do you know?

CHORUS
Oh, lordy, by self experience.

ELIJAH McCOY
Excuse me, I'm…

RAILWAY WORKER
How do you know?

CHORUS
Oh, lordy!

> *Actor #3 sits on a crate in the background, back to the*
> *stage. ELIJAH walks up to the SECRETARY. Actor #7*
> *looks over crates. Actor #6 exits.*

ELIJAH McCOY
Excuse me I'm looking for the offices of the Michigan Central
Railroad?

SECRETARY
Can I help you, sugah?

ELIJAH McCOY
Yes, I'm here to see Mr. Golrokh.

SECRETARY
One moment please.

Enter MR. GOLROKH.

MR. GOLROKH
May I help you?

ELIJAH McCOY
I'm Mr. Rankine's apprentice. Elijah McCoy. I'm here for the engineering position.

MR. GOLROKH
Oh, you've got to be joking.

ELIJAH McCOY
No sir, I'm not.

MR. GOLROKH
Let me get this straight, you were Mr. Rankine's apprentice?

ELIJAH McCOY
That is correct sir.

MR. GOLROKH
What's his middle name?

ELIJAH McCOY
John Macquorn. His most important work; *Manual of the Steam Engine and other Prime Movers*. In it, he writes of the Law of Conservation of Energy which states all different kinds of physical energy in the universe are mutually convertible. Elected Fellow of the Royal Society in 1853. Shall I go on?

MR. GOLROKH
Awwh.

ELIJAH McCOY
I moved here on the prospect of employment. What do you expect me to do?

MR. GOLROKH
Oh, I haven't got the slightest clue. Good day.

MR. GOLROKH leaves. DON turns around on his crate.

DON BOGIE
Psst. Hey, you boy. Comeer. Where the hell are you from?

ELIJAH McCOY
I beg your pardon.

DON BOGIE
"I beg your pardon" I said, where the hell you from?

ELIJAH McCOY
Colchester, Upper Canada.

DON BOGIE
Name's Donbogie. First name Don, last name Bogie, everyone round here calls me Donbogie.

ELIJAH McCOY
Well, Don Bogie, it's good to meet…

DON BOGIE
Yeah, boy, enough with the frou frou, you need a job.

ELIJAH McCOY
I can find a job.

DON BOGIE
Yeah, yeah. Listen. You show up at this address. They'll get you a job.

ELIJAH McCOY
Thanks.

DON BOGIE
Don't be thankin me for nothin see cause I gets a commission. Now get yourself some sleep cause you sure as hell look like you need it.

DON exits singing "Chesapeake Bay." ROMULUS and REMUS enter.

ROMULUS
And then the boxer says, "Isn't she the one with the donkey in the attic?"

They both laugh very hard. ELIJAH enters.

REMUS
Don't do that to me!

ROMULUS
Donkey in the…

ELIJAH McCOY
Excuse me, gentlemen.

REMUS
You're killing me!

ROMULUS
In the attic!

REMUS
You're killing me!

ELIJAH McCOY
Excuse me.

ROMULUS
Maybe there's a rooster in the basement!

REMUS
Stop! Stop! Oh, God!

ELIJAH McCOY
Excuse me, gentlemen!

REMUS
May I help you?

ELIJAH McCOY
I was told, by a mister Don Bogie that I could find
employment here.

ROMULUS
All we got left is grease monkey.

ELIJAH McCOY
I don't think so.

ROMULUS
Then what are you doing here?

ELIJAH McCOY

Surely there must be a position in the office… filing clerk.

ROMULUS

Heh, a Negro filing clerk. Heh. Right.

> *ELIJAH starts to walk away.*

ELIJAH McCOY

Oh, for heaven's sake, this is the most frustrating…

REMUS

Woah, woah, woah, woah! Fireman. You could stoke the boiler as well as oilman. Little bit more pay.

ROMULUS

You know, we have important things to do other than sit here and wait for you to make up your mind.

ELIJAH McCOY

Well then I suppose I should… I should get to work.

> *He looks around the stage and starts to work. NANNY HUBBARD enters with GEORGE, reading a letter.*

NANNY HUBBARD

I am happy to hear that you have found work in the land of the free and the home of the brave.

GEORGE McCOY

Don't you dare put down anything in regards to me.

NANNY HUBBARD

Your father is very proud of you and wishes you the best of luck.

GEORGE McCOY

I ain't speakin to that boy till I hear an apology.

NANNY HUBBARD

I think however, he may still have some sore feelings about some of the things you said to him before you left.

GEORGE McCOY

He wants to be on his own, let him be on his own!

NANNY HUBBARD

I know you're busy, but it would be nice to hear from you. And if you could slip in a little apology to your father, all the better. Love, your Nanny Hubbard.

> *Actor #6 enters with letter from ELIJAH. He gives her the letter and takes NANNY HUBBARD's letter from her and exits.*

ELIJAH McCOY

Dear Nan, I was so glad to hear from you. Things are going as well as can be expected. As for Father, I will apologize for hurting his feelings, but I cannot apologize for my beliefs. My father taught me to work hard, to never give up, open my eyes, and I have. God made man an imperfect thing. I don't have that luxury. This world, made by the Lord God almighty, is full of injustice, cruelty and pain.

GEORGE McCOY

Stop reading.

ELIJAH McCOY

Inefficiencies abound. Waste abounds. Mistakes that cost lives. That reward the cruel. That punish the pure of spirit. My dear mother, a woman of goodness and piety…

GEORGE McCOY

Stop reading.

ELIJAH McCOY

…would be alive today had it not been for His divine incompetence. With each passing day I grow more and more sure that His great bounty and wisdom is nothing but a cruel and impetuous…

GEORGE McCOY

Give me the goddamned…

ELIJAH McCOY

Cynical, practical joke at the expense of…

> *GEORGE takes the letter from NANNY HUBBARD and tears it apart.*

NANNY HUBBARD

George.

GEORGE McCOY

No. That man, he's not my son. That man is not my son.

> *GEORGE exits. NANNY HUBBARD picks up torn letter and exits. ELIJAH works on the engine. MRS. ELENORA LLOYD enters with DON.*

MRS. ELENORA LLOYD

No, YOU listen here! I have to be at my destination no later than quarter past three.

DON BOGIE

I's sorry ma'am, but we are not scheduled to arrive until four ten. Now, if you will take your seat.

MRS. ELENORA LLOYD

But why are we stopped?!

DON BOGIE

With all due respect ma'am, have you not taken a train before?

MRS. ELENORA LLOYD

What does that matter?!

DON BOGIE

We gots to stop the train every ten miles or so, to grease up all the parts, so that we can keep on going to our destination.

MRS. ELENORA LLOYD

You must be mad.

DON BOGIE

No ma'am.

MRS. ELENORA LLOYD

You mean we will be stopping this train every ten miles?!

DON BOGIE

It's a nice chance to get to know the countryside, now if you'll take your seat.

MRS. ELENORA LLOYD

You, Negro. YOU THERE!

ELIJAH McCOY
> May I help you?

MRS. ELENORA LLOYD
> I want you to stop what you're doing, right this second and get in that contraption and start this train.

ELIJAH McCOY
> I would love to be able to do that, but I can't. Second law of thermodynamics.

MRS. ELENORA LLOYD
> Why that is the… do you have any idea who I am young man?

ELIJAH McCOY
> Someone who obviously hasn't the slightest clue about the complexities of a modern steam engine, now go back to your seat before I take this spanner and brain you with it.

MRS. ELENORA LLOYD
> You watch your tongue, Negro, you hear me!

ELIJAH McCOY
> I hear you. Get back on the train.

> *MRS. ELENORA LLOYD leaves.*

DON BOGIE
> Listen here McCoy! You can feel all uppity and superior to me and the rest of the Negroes, but whatever you do, you do not speak to White people like that or you're gonna get yourself killed, you hear me?

ELIJAH McCOY
> I don't think I'm superior to you.

DON BOGIE
> Listen here, this Friday night, church around the corner's throwing a kind of get together pot luck, you're gonna come with me, you understand?

ELIJAH McCOY
> You ever thought about post-secondary education?

DON BOGIE
>Negro, please.

>>*All the other actors appear onstage as a church congregation, they set up the church.*

CHORUS
>REJOICE, REJOICE. EMMANUEL SHALL COME TO THEE O ISRAEL.

ELIJAH McCOY
>That doorway is a fire hazard.

DON BOGIE
>Would you be quiet.

ELIJAH McCOY
>Where's the food, I'm starving.

DON BOGIE
>I ain't funnin with you now.

>>*REVEREND WALKER takes the pulpit. During the sermon, ANNE looks at ELIJAH.*

REVEREND WALKER
>And the Lord hath said unto man, many times, you are too proudful! You are too big for your britches. But the Lord has a way of taking you down a peg. And be mindful of your arrogance, for the vengeance of God is terrible and absolute. Now, let's all make Sister Mary proud and eat all the food she laid out for us here tonight.

EVERYONE
>Amen.

>>*DON walks towards the food. ELIJAH pulls him back.*

ELIJAH McCOY
>Donbogie.

DON BOGIE
>Now, look here, you just best hand over them ham hocks right this here second.

ELIJAH McCOY
> Donbogie.

DON BOGIE
> Damn your blood and guts, this here is some fine eats.

ELIJAH McCOY
> That girl. Over there.

DON BOGIE
> Who?

ELIJAH McCOY
> What's her name.

DON BOGIE
> The hell should I know.

ELIJAH McCOY
> Introduce me to her.

DON BOGIE
> You listen here, a damn second McCoy. This is America,
> I don't give a damn what they get up to where you come
> from, but here, you're on your own.

ELIJAH McCOY
> Fair enough.

> > *ELIJAH walks over to ANNE who is sitting with
> > a friend. DON, Actors #3, #6 and #7 exit.*

ANNE ELIZABETH STEWART
> Now, of course the first impression I had was that...

ELIJAH McCOY
> I'm terribly sorry to bother you, but you seem very familiar,
> my name is Elijah McCoy, engineer. Have we met?

ANNE ELIZABETH STEWART
> No, but I knew you were going to ask me that question.

> *Actor #5 exits.*

ELIJAH McCOY
> That so.

She extends her hand.

ANNE ELIZABETH STEWART
Anne Elizabeth Stewart.

ELIJAH McCOY
Pleasure to make your acquaintance.

ANNE ELIZABETH STEWART
I can't quite place that accent.

ELIJAH McCOY
Colchester, Upper Canada. Born and raised.

ANNE ELIZABETH STEWART
I see.

ELIJAH McCOY
Would I be too forward in asking you to walk with me for a spell?

ANNE ELIZABETH STEWART
Fortunately, you would not.

They walk. Light up on NANNY HUBBARD.

NANNY HUBBARD
Elijah, I realize you're very busy, but I really do think that you should drop a quick message to your father. He has not been well lately and I really and truly believe that he would benefit a great deal upon hearing a response from you.

ANNE ELIZABETH STEWART
No actually I'm from Mercer County, Kentucky.

ELIJAH McCOY
My folks are from Kentucky.

ANNE ELIZABETH STEWART
You're from good stock.

GEORGE lays down. NANNY HUBBARD lays a blanket on him. Kisses his forehead.

NANNY HUBBARD
I am not trying to be a bother…

ELIJAH McCOY
> And then my father joined the Royal Upper Canadian Army, served during the 1837 rebellion…

ANNE ELIZABETH STEWART
> I see.

ELIJAH McCOY
> The way he tells it, he practically held Mackenzie in his sights when he was ordered to stand down.

NANNY HUBBARD
> But I implore you…

> *ANNE laughs, then coughs.*

ANNE ELIZABETH STEWART
> Pardon.

ELIJAH McCOY
> Sounds to me like you're catching cold. Shall we go in?

> *She kisses him on the cheek.*

ANNE ELIZABETH STEWART
> And now you have it too.

> *ANNE exits.*

NANNY HUBBARD
> If you have any love left in your heart for the man who gave you life…

ELIJAH McCOY
> I am very sorry it has taken me this long to respond to your letters. I have no other excuse than the idleness that accompanies a deep frustration and lack of fulfillment. As for the long awaited atonement, it is forthcoming. I formally offer my sincere and heartfelt apologies to my father for my previous rantings and outbursts. No doubt he will question the veracity of my capitulation, but I can give you proof. I am in LOVE! Her name is Anne Elizabeth Stewart, and she has dulled the knife point of my youthful dementia. I cannot wait to put harsh words behind us and for you to meet the woman I intend to marry. Your son. Elijah.

NANNY HUBBARD

Dear, Elijah, I regret to inform you... I regretfully...

> *Actor #6 places a bowl of water on stage. ELIJAH grabs the letter out of NANNY HUBBARD's hand. Reads it as he exits through the trap door. GEORGE walks up to the bowl of water. Dips his hands in and baptizes himself.*

CHORUS

REJOICE, REJOICE. EMMANUELLE SHALL COME TO THEE, O ISRAEL.

GEORGE McCOY

One of the hardest things I've had to do in my life, was let that boy cry himself to sleep. If you keep picking up the child, he'll never get to sleep on his own. But the night is so dark, and every living creature knows that fear of solitude. I just wanted to ease the child a bit, but that wouldn't make him a man. That wouldn't make him a man.

> *ELIJAH opens the trap door. He's hard at work. ANNE enters with a tray of tea and a sandwich and a pie. DON knocks on the door.*

ANNE ELIZABETH STEWART

The door is open. How'd it go?

DON BOGIE

Well, I spoke with them again and I'm sorry but the answer is the same. They don't give time off to Negroes for a death in the family.

ANNE ELIZABETH STEWART

I hate to say, I'm not surprised but...

DON BOGIE

Elijah here?

ANNE ELIZABETH STEWART

Downstairs. Can I get you something?

DON BOGIE

No thanks, Miss Stewart.

ANNE ELIZABETH STEWART
Now, Don, how many times do I…

DON BOGIE
Mrs. McCoy.

ANNE ELIZABETH STEWART
Anne. Call me Anne.

DON BOGIE
Mrs. Anne. How's that.

She calls down to ELIJAH.

ANNE ELIZABETH STEWART
Honey, Don's here. Come on up darling.

ELIJAH enters, lost in thought.

ELIJAH McCOY
James Watt took the Newcomen engine and added 2
cylinders.

DON BOGIE
Who's he talkin to…

ANNE ELIZABETH STEWART
Don't you pay him no mind and have this here glass of
lemonade.

ELIJAH McCOY
One hot, one cold. Sun and planet gearing system.

DON BOGIE
Been like this for long?

ANNE ELIZABETH STEWART
All night and well into the morning for he goes to work.

ELIJAH McCOY
Then came Richard Trevithick. Watt said he "deserved
hanging." You old dog. You madman. You ripped the
condensers right off, shooting steam straight into the waaaait
a second.

ELIJAH takes his note pad and draws furiously.

ELIJAH McCOY
Donbogie, come here please!

DON goes to ELIJAH.

DON BOGIE
Yes sir.

ELIJAH McCOY
Look at this.

DON BOGIE
Good googly goo.

ELIJAH McCOY
Newcomen revolutionized the steam engine by adding self regulating valves. I've taken that idea and applied it to the entire oil system.

DON BOGIE
You put the oil in here…

ELIJAH McCOY
And it goes through the entire system.

DON BOGIE
You'd never have to leave the cabin.

ELIJAH McCOY
That is correct.

DON BOGIE
What about the…

ELIJAH McCOY
Each piston has a small groove. See.

DON BOGIE
Good Lord.

ELIJAH McCOY
What's the average time it takes to stop the train, oil it up, get it on its way.

DON BOGIE
Twenty five minutes rain, fifteen minutes dry.

ELIJAH McCOY
> Now, using a best guess, how much time could you shave
> from the average oil stop using this device.

DON BOGIE
> You mean if we had this system…

ELIJAH McCOY
> In every train. How much time could we save from every
> stop we make.

DON BOGIE
> I would say, and this is just a guess, but if we didn't have to
> leave the cabin, we just put oil in here and it goes through
> the entire system, I would say we could do the entire engine
> in five, ten minutes tops.

ELIJAH McCOY
> Excellent.

> *ELIJAH tears up his drawings.*

DON BOGIE
> The hell are you doing!?

ELIJAH McCOY
> The train must never stop.

DON BOGIE
> The train must never stop?

ELIJAH McCOY
> The train… must never… stop.

DON BOGIE
> You're a mad man.

ELIJAH McCOY
> I am the alpha and omega!

> *ELIJAH enters the trap.*

ANNE ELIZABETH STEWART
> Bumble Berry Pie?

DON BOGIE
> Sho nuff.

ANNE ELIZABETH STEWART
Now, Donbogie, I have to ask you a very important question.

DON BOGIE
I have never had an affair with a married woman, no, but I am a young man...

ANNE ELIZABETH STEWART
Listen, I want you to tell me about the men you work for.

DON BOGIE
What about them.

ANNE ELIZABETH STEWART
Elijah's thinking about approaching them when he's done.

DON BOGIE
I see.

ANNE ELIZABETH STEWART
Is there anybody else in this town who might be able to help him out with the business end of things?

DON BOGIE
In what way?

ANNE places a sandwich on stage.

ANNE ELIZABETH STEWART
He needs a good business partner. I saw the way my father ran his church and it is very important, even for a man of the cloth to have good business partners. I was thinking that...

DON BOGIE
Mrs. McCoy...

ANNE ELIZABETH STEWART
Anne.

DON BOGIE
I don't think you understand...

ELIJAH enters.

ELIJAH McCOY
My darling, I'm sorry to bother you, but...

ANNE ELIZABETH STEWART
Your tea's on the counter.

ELIJAH McCOY
Thank you, my sweet.

> *He goes to get his tea. ANNE and DON are on the other side of the stage.*

ANNE ELIZABETH STEWART
Now, do you have any connections in our community... someone who could help him develop a good business plan...

DON BOGIE
Listen. Okay, Anne, this here is fun and all, and I don't mind bein a part of it, but... no Black man in this town has the kind of money he's gonna need, if he's successful...

ANNE ELIZABETH STEWART
Oh, he'll be successful.

> *The steam engine revs faster.*

DON BOGIE
No White man in this town is gonna give a Black man the kind of capital he's gonna need if he's successful...

ANNE ELIZABETH STEWART
What about if...

> *ELIJAH notices that there's a hole in his tea cup.*

DON BOGIE
Anne... I have worked in this business for the past ten years, since I was fifteen. I have worked trains from Tennessee to Rhode Island. I know trains. Every inch. There ain't no way, not on God's green earth, that you can make a train travel from one city to the next and not have to stop and oil up. No White man can do it, no Black man can do it. Not on God's green earth.

ELIJAH McCOY
There's a hole!

ANNE ELIZABETH STEWART
Oh, I keep forgetting to toss that damn thing away.

She takes the cup from him. He grabs her.

What's the matter?

ELIJAH McCOY
There's a hole.

He kisses her.

I love you more than life itself!

He runs to DON.

Donbogie!

DON BOGIE
Right here.

ELIJAH tosses a set of keys to DON.

ELIJAH McCOY
Get to the B17 tool shed, I'm going to need the 5 and
a quarter inch copper drill.

DON BOGIE
I was just about to get my pie.

ELIJAH pushes DON out the door.

ELIJAH McCOY
I will buy you every pie from here to Washington state if you
just do as I say.

DON BOGIE
No rest for the wicked.

DON exits.

ELIJAH McCOY
I can feel his hand slipping.

ANNE ELIZABETH STEWART
I love you.

ELIJAH McCOY
The cosmos will be ours.

ELIJAH enters the trap and slams the door. ROMULUS and REMUS enter. ROMULUS goes to the sandwich that ANNE left on the set and spends the entire scene trying to eat it.

ROMULUS

Oh, you've lost your mind!

REMUS

Last year, it wasn't at the estate, it was at the cottage. You and Dad promised…

ROMULUS

You're delusional.

DON knocks at the door.

REMUS

You'd let me have *Queenie,* for June and July.

ROMULUS

There is no way I'd let you have *Queenie* for June and July.

DON knocks again.

REMUS

Not now, Don.

ROMULUS

Take the schooner.

REMUS

Don't want the schooner, I want *Queenie.*

ROMULUS

You've never sailed *Queenie* before.

REMUS

Yes I have.

DON knocks again.

ROMULUS

Don, are you deaf, or are you stupid. We're having a conversation.

DON BOGIE

Terribly sorry to bother you sah. I just got myself something here that I think you should see.

> *DON inches into the room with a model steam engine under his arm.*

ROMULUS

Well, I don't want to see it, I'm having a very important business discussion with my brother about very important things and you are not to disobey me, now, take what ever it is you have and get out.

> *He shoves DON away.*

You've never sailed *Queenie* before. You don't know how to handle her...

> *DON knocks.*

I swear to God, Donbogie, I'm gonna smack you across the skull so hard...

DON BOGIE

I am so sorry to be disturbing you suh, but I really really think that this here is something you really ought to see. It is the most astonishing thing... I really don't know what to say, but please...

REMUS

Let him in, let him in.

DON BOGIE

Thank you, thank you, suh.

REMUS

Now, what seems to be the problem?

DON BOGIE

Suh, you needs to take a look at this.

> *He puts the model on the table.*

ROMULUS

What is it.

DON BOGIE

It is a mock up of a DM&IR 221 engine. These babies can pull a full load of iron ore uphill and backwards.

ROMULUS

Yes.

DON BOGIE

This here engine, you got to oil every piece for a full hour and a half before it can work for twenty minutes.

ROMULUS

Your point?

DON BOGIE

Well, suh, Mr. McCoy, he found a way to keep her oiled while she's running.

ROMULUS

I don't understand what that means.

DON BOGIE

Sir, he's invented this here cup, that takes the steam from the engine and uses it to pump oil through the engine continuously, so that she never has to stop.

ROMULUS

Oh, good Lord, Don, don't waste my time!

DON BOGIE

I am serious suh.

ROMULUS

It is impossible to keep a locomotive lubricated while it... see this is something... Don, we're the... this is something you don't quite understand okay?

DON BOGIE

Suh, I have seen this thing in action and...

ROMULUS

I don't care what you've seen. It's a hoax. You've been duped. Now, get the hell out of here and take that contraption with you!

DON BOGIE

But, suh…

ROMULUS

No but, suh, get the hell out before I actually start to get angry for real. And you don't want to see that.

He shoves DON out of the room.

REMUS

What are you doing.

ROMULUS

What do you mean what am I doing?

REMUS

Do you understand that this is exactly what Mother means when she says you'd cut off your nose to spite your face.

ROMULUS

No it is not.

REMUS

Don.

ROMULUS

You obviously don't even know what the phrase means.

REMUS

Don, you still there.

DON BOGIE

Yes, suh.

REMUS

Could you come back in please.

DON inches in the room.

DON BOGIE

Yes, suh.

REMUS

You've seen this thing in action.

DON BOGIE

Yes, I have suh.

REMUS
Do you think it's a hoax.

DON BOGIE
I'm not quite sure if I know what that word means suh.

REMUS
Do you think he's trying to pull a fast one?

DON BOGIE
No, suh.

REMUS
You say that with great authority.

DON BOGIE
Suh... I know how crazy this must sound, coming out the mouth of a Negro and all, but suh, this is the real deal.

REMUS
Well, leave it here and you can tell Mr. McCoy we will meet with him in our office first thing tomorrow morning.

DON BOGIE
Suh, he's right outside.

REMUS
Oh, well, I suppose we should let him in.

DON BOGIE
Elijah!

> *ELIJAH walks confidently into the room with a small wooden box, a pillow, a book and his glasses under his arm.*

ELIJAH McCOY
Gentlemen, good day to you, or perhaps I should say good evening.

REMUS
Elijah.

ROMULUS
Donbogie here tells us that you have revolutionized the steam engine.

ELIJAH McCOY

Well, I don't know about that just yet. I only have
a prototype, a full scale engine would have to be built
and tested and perfected, but what I think I have is the
beginning of a whole new level of efficiency for American
business.

ROMULUS

Well, that's very optimistic.

> *ELIJAH puts the box down. Pulls out each item as he
> mentions them.*

ELIJAH McCOY

I have brought matches, a container of oil and water. There is
a small amount of coal that should burn for the better part of
three hours. As long as you keep the boiler full of coal, and
the cup full of oil, it will run without seizing.

ROMULUS

Well, thank you very...

ELIJAH McCOY

I have brought my reading glasses, a pillow and a good
book.

REMUS

You're well prepared.

> *Takes ELIJAH's book.*

ROMULUS

What's this?

ELIJAH McCOY

*On the Thermodynamic Theory of Waves of Finite Longitudinal
Disturbance* by William Rankine.

ROMULUS

Well, that's... that's pretty heavy reading.

ELIJAH McCOY

Yes, there are no pretty pictures, otherwise I'd lend you
a copy.

ROMULUS
Say…

REMUS
Brother, you coming?

> *ELIJAH takes the book from ROMULUS. REMUS hands ROMULUS the sandwich. ROMULUS leaves. REMUS smiles at ELIJAH, follows his brother with everything else.*

DON BOGIE
You gonna be okay without me?

ELIJAH McCOY
I'll be just fine.

DON BOGIE
Elijah, let me just say… I'm very proud to be a part of this whole thing here.

> *DON shakes ELIJAH's hand.*

ELIJAH McCOY
Don.

DON BOGIE
Yes, suh.

ELIJAH McCOY
There is a college…

DON BOGIE
Alright, alright…

ELIJAH McCOY
…just two blocks away from the station.

DON BOGIE
Let go my hand.

ELIJAH McCOY
Promise me you'll just check out the courses you think you can afford.

DON BOGIE
I said let go of my damn hand.

DON exits.

ELIJAH McCOY
Where's my Anna Bella!

ANNE ELIZABETH STEWART
I'm in here!

ANNE enters from offstage.

ELIJAH McCOY
Can I tell you a secret?

ANNE ELIZABETH STEWART
They loved it.

ELIJAH McCOY
I swear to God, I wish you could have seen their faces!

He swings her around.

ANNE ELIZABETH STEWART
Oh, I knew you could do it!

ELIJAH McCOY
Did you now.

ANNE ELIZABETH STEWART
Last night I dreamt, I was walking though a desert and my skin was on fire.

ELIJAH McCOY
Go on.

ELIJAH holds her close. ANNE uses the dream to seduce ELIJAH.

ANNE ELIZABETH STEWART
You were standing before me and your body was made of water. And when we touched, the flames burned hotter and hotter…

ELIJAH McCOY
It's a sign. Water is a sign of good luck.

He kisses her neck.

ANNE ELIZABETH STEWART
Yes, it is.

She coughs.

ELIJAH McCOY
Let me get you a glass of water.

ANNE ELIZABETH STEWART
No, I'm fine.

ELIJAH McCOY
Please, my darling, you are my muse, I must treat my muse
with utter care and servitude.

*She pulls him to a chair. He sits and pulls her onto his
lap.*

ANNE ELIZABETH STEWART
Listen to me, do not take the first offer they make.

ELIJAH McCOY
My dear, I have a plan.

ANNE ELIZABETH STEWART
You get a contract, you bring it home to me. We'll take a look
at it together.

He kisses her. Deep, slow, passionate.

ELIJAH McCOY
You are my Euphrates! My Ariadne!

ANNE ELIZABETH STEWART
I know.

ROMULUS and REMUS enter. ANNE exits.

REMUS
Yeah, like I'm going to let you do all the talking.

ROMULUS
I'm serious, this could be very…

ELIJAH knocks on the door.

ROMULUS
Come in, Mr. McCoy.

ELIJAH McCOY
Gentlemen.

ROMULUS
Close the door behind you, please.

> *He does.*

REMUS
Thank you for...

ROMULUS
Listen here, boy, where the hell did you steal this from!

ELIJAH McCOY
I beg your pardon.

ROMULUS
No Negro could have created this lubricating cup. It's not possible. You stole it. We want to know who you stole it from.

REMUS
Is there any way that you could prove that you invented this... device?

ELIJAH McCOY
Would my registered patent serve as proof.

> *ELIJAH pulls out the patent.*

REMUS
You have a patent.

ELIJAH McCOY
Yes. I do.

> *REMUS takes it from ELIJAH. ROMULUS takes it from REMUS. REMUS takes it from ROMULUS. ROMULUS takes it from REMUS. REMUS takes it from ROMULUS and points at ROMULUS as if to say "stop screwing around." REMUS sits with the patent and starts to read.*

ROMULUS
How does it work?

ELIJAH McCOY

I beg your pardon?

ROMULUS

You invented it, you should be able to explain how it works.

> *ANNE looks at a projection of the device projected on the stage.*

ELIJAH McCOY

Lubricating cup. Oil filled reservoir here. A hollow tube extends from the…

ANNE ELIZABETH STEWART

…bottom of the cup…

ELIJAH McCOY

…down into the chamber of the steam engine.

ANNE ELIZABETH STEWART

Steam rises up…

ELIJAH McCOY

…from the engine activating this piston.

REMUS

Releasing oil from the reservoir…

ANNE ELIZABETH STEWART

Steam.

ELIJAH McCOY

Into the cylinder of the engine.

ANNE ELIZABETH STEWART

Water caught in the midst of its own obliteration.

REMUS

How do you regulate the steam, so that it doesn't blast out all of the oil?

ELIJAH McCOY

Stopcock.

REMUS

Of course.

ANNE ELIZABETH STEWART
One would hope that water is at peace with its fate.

REMUS
It's so simple.

ANNE ELIZABETH STEWART
How awful it would be, in the final moment, to struggle against the inevitable.

REMUS
It's so simple.

ROMULUS and REMUS exit. ANNE starts coughing.

ELIJAH McCOY
Anna! Anna!!! I have a contract! I haven't signed it yet I...

DON enters.

DON BOGIE
Now, don't be mad.

ELIJAH McCOY
What's going on.

DON BOGIE
I gave a call to Sistah Matilda. She got some special teas and such. She'll be here any minute.

ELIJAH McCOY
Where's Anne.

DON BOGIE
Now, hold on a second.

He finds ANNE.

ELIJAH McCOY
Oh. My God!

DON BOGIE
I got some water on the boil, and...

ELIJAH McCOY
There's so much blood...

DON BOGIE
Now, she didn't want to be a bother to you cause of your meeting and all, so…

ELIJAH McCOY
Honey, we… we have to get you to a hospital. Yes we do.

ANNE shakes her head.

DON BOGIE
Help is on the way, now just…

ELIJAH picks her up in his arms.

ELIJAH McCOY
Don't… just… get out of my way.

DON BOGIE
But if you…

ELIJAH McCOY
Don, get the hell out of my way.

DR. GRANT enters.

DR. GRANT
This is a White man's hospital, you know you can't bring her in here!

ELIJAH McCOY
But it's the closest one, I don't have time to…

DR. GRANT
There is a Negro hospital…

ELIJAH McCOY
It's on the other side of town.

DR. GRANT
You know where it is, good.

DR. GRANT exits, DR. TILLY enters.

DR. TILLY
She has a cold.

ELIJAH McCOY
She doesn't have a cold. It's more serious than that.

DR. TILLY
We don't have the beds, and if we did, we don't have the staff.

ELIJAH McCOY
You listen to me!

DR. TILLY
Sir, let go of my arm!

ELIJAH McCOY
She is my wife, I have to do something.

DR. TILLY
Keep the windows open, perhaps some fresh air.

ELIJAH McCOY
What if she's dying!

DR. TILLY
Then I suggest you make arrangements.

> *DR. TILLY walks away. DON appears.*

DON BOGIE
Bring her over here. Elijah?

ELIJAH McCOY
Sorry?

DON BOGIE
Bring her here.

ELIJAH McCOY
Uh… yes. Uhm…

> *SISTER MATILDA enters.*

DON BOGIE
Sistah, I'd like you to meet…

SISTER MATILDA
We all got time for that later. Show me to the kitchen please.

ELIJAH McCOY
It's right behind…

> *He points, she leaves with ANNE.*

DON BOGIE
Not to worry, she's in good hands now. The best.

ELIJAH McCOY
Don, I don't think she's getting any better.

DON BOGIE
Don't you think that way, she gonna be fine. Just fine.

> *Music. ELIJAH sits, alone. He takes off his glasses.*

ACT TWO

> *Lights up. ROMULUS and REMUS enter with a bottle of champagne.*

REMUS
It's the region.

ROMULUS
It's the type of grape.

REMUS
No it's not.

ROMULUS
The champagne grape.

REMUS
You know, I'm not sure what's more annoying, willful ignorance, or stupidity.

ROMULUS
Willful ignorance. Definitely.

> *ELIJAH knocks at the door.*

REMUS
Come in.

ELIJAH McCOY
Gentleman.

ROMULUS
You were able to look over the contract?

ELIJAH McCOY
Yes, I was.

REMUS
Now, I know we were only offering a total of a thousand dollars, but that is really the best offer we could…

ELIJAH McCOY
It's fine.

REMUS
It's fine?

ELIJAH McCOY
I'd like to get to work. There's still lots to do.

REMUS
Uh, yes well.

> *ROMULUS goes to the cheque book.*

ROMULUS
I know we were supposed to have a five hundred dollar payment today, but we seem to be having a bit of a cash flow problem. Will one hundred be okay, just for now? We're good for it.

ELIJAH McCOY
Fine.

REMUS
Are you okay, you seem…

ELIJAH McCOY
My wife died last night.

> *ANNE enters with a bowl of water. She baptizes herself.*

ROMULUS
Oh. I'm… I'm so sorry.

REMUS
I am so sorry to hear of your loss.

ELIJAH McCOY
It's fine. We have a lot of work to do, so let's get to it.

ROMULUS pulls out cash.

ROMULUS
Tell you what… two hundred… let's make that… as a matter of fact, you know what? We'll just deal with the cash flow situation some other way. Here you go.

Hands over money.

ELIJAH McCOY
Thank you sir.

REMUS
We'll see you downstairs.

ELIJAH McCOY
Yes.

ELIJAH leaves.

REMUS
What are you doing?!

ROMULUS
The man's wife just died.

REMUS
We still have to find six hundred dollars from…

ROMULUS
Give it a rest wouldja…

ELIJAH enters and stands on stage. His breathing is deep and erratic. He is having a nervous breakdown. DON enters, watches for a bit.

DON BOGIE
Elijah?

ELIJAH stops suddenly. Surprised. Unsure of what DON saw.

ELIJAH
Yes, Don.

DON BOGIE
I ain't disturbin you or nuthin am I?

ELIJAH lies.

ELIJAH McCOY

Controlled breathing. Two minutes, three times a day. Improves circulation. Come in. Come in.

He performs his "controlled breathing."

DON BOGIE

I just talked with Reverend Walker, there seems to be some kind of problem with the family.

ELIJAH McCOY

Yes?

DON BOGIE

She's got some folks want her to be buried back down in Kentucky. Now, as far as the reverend is concerned, it's your call, but sounds to me like...

ELIJAH laughs a little.

DON BOGIE

What's so funny?

ELIJAH McCOY

Can you imagine how efficiently one could live one's life, if you could travel backwards and forwards in time.

DON BOGIE

Well, I suppose.

ELIJAH McCOY

If things move forward in time, they must also be able to move backwards. All one would really have to do is break the problem down into its component parts, commit one's self to some initial experiments, sketch out an approach.

DON BOGIE

Listen here. Elijah. You gonna be alright.

ELIJAH McCOY

Oh, I know I will. I will.

MR. PARKS enters with MR. BURGESS.

MR. WILBUR GABRIEL PARKS
Somebody get me a glass of damn water!

MR. BURGESS
Spector Manufacturing increased their productivity by 45%, we can't afford not to...

> *MR. PARKS glances occasionally at ELIJAH.*

MR. WILBUR GABRIEL PARKS
I do not give a flying budgie's petard what the hell Spector whatsit is doin! Listen here, if we need some kind of lubricatin cup we will find one, but I will be strung up naked before the ghost of General George E. Pickett if this company ever, ever threatens its... I mean, are you thinkin about what you're saying?

MR. BURGESS
This company can't afford...

MR. WILBUR GABRIEL PARKS
Now, get me a damn glass of water before I tear your skin off your bones with my own goddamned teeth and throw your bloody carcass to a pack of toothless mountain lions.

> *MR. PARKS exits.*

MR. BURGESS
Mary!

> *MARY enters.*

MARY ELEANORA DELANEY
Yes, Mr. Burgess?

MR. BURGESS
A glass of water for Mr. Parks.

MARY ELEANORA DELANEY
Right away, Mr. Burgess.

> *MARY exits.*

MR. BURGESS
Mr. McCoy, may I talk to you for a second.

ELIJAH McCOY
>If there's a problem with…

MR. BURGESS
>I am so sorry, sir, but I don't think, at this time that we will be able to…

ELIJAH McCOY
>I can assure you, if you are concerned about the verisimilitude of my claims…

MR. BURGESS
>It's not… in…

ELIJAH McCOY
>I have brought with me…

MR. BURGESS
>That won't be…

ELIJAH McCOY
>If you need…

MR. BURGESS
>I can't help you Mr. McCoy. I'm sorry. I can't.

ELIJAH McCOY
>No, Mr. Burgess. It is I who is unable to help you.

>>*MARY returns.*

MR. BURGESS
>Yes. Yes. Well. Goodbye.

>>*MR. BURGESS extends his hand. ELIJAH shakes it.*
>>*MR. BURGESS exits. MARY runs after ELIJAH.*

MARY ELEANORA DELANEY
>Mr. McCoy! Mr. McCoy!

ELIJAH McCOY
>Will it never end.

MARY ELEANORA DELANEY
>I uhm… I should introduce myself. My name is Mary Eleanora Delaney and I was hoping that I could speak to you for a moment.

ELIJAH McCOY
Yes?

MARY ELEANORA DELANEY
I am a member of a group that encourages our youth by providing inspirational speakers at a local church every Thursday and Friday night. And I was hoping to enlist your services.

ELIJAH McCOY
I don't know if I can help you, I have to get back to...

MARY ELEANORA DELANEY
Oh, I don't mean tonight.

ELIJAH McCOY
Ah.

MARY ELEANORA DELANEY
I do, however need to talk to you Mr. McCoy about when and how we could get you back here to Detroit and your accommodation.

ELIJAH McCOY
I'm very busy...

> *ROMULUS and REMUS enter the stage.*

REMUS
McCoy!

MARY ELEANORA DELANEY
My card.

REMUS
Office, please!

ELIJAH McCOY
Well, Mary... Eleanora? I will consider the invitation.

MARY ELEANORA DELANEY
It has been an honour to meet you, Mr. McCoy.

> *She leaves.*

ROMULUS
I'll talk to him.

REMUS
I'll talk to him.

ROMULUS
Let me talk to him.

REMUS
Stay out of this, I mean it.

ELIJAH enters.

ELIJAH McCOY
Gentlemen.

REMUS
Why on earth does it matter to you if our clients know that you're a Negro or not.

ELIJAH McCOY
I believe very strongly that it is important to...

REMUS
You see this?!

ELIJAH McCOY
You have a tendency...

REMUS
Cancelled invoices.

He throws a pile of paper at ELIJAH.

ELIJAH McCOY
Very well.

REMUS
Thousands of thousands of dollars.

ELIJAH McCOY
I am not ashamed of who I am and I will not be made to lie.

REMUS
Do you not care if we make money. Is this some kind of...

ROMULUS
May I say something.

REMUS
> You're a very smart man. You have got to learn to listen. This company needs to create REVENUE. That's how companies work.

ELIJAH McCOY
> I realize that.

REMUS
> No you do not!!! Nor do you understand what is in your best interest. In business, you put your personal interests aside for the sake of the company. I put up with your capricious exorbitant demands for exotic materials, I understand that God made man imperfect, but you have to get through that thick skull of yours that this enterprise cannot sustain itself if every client I bring through that door, you send to the competition!

> *ROMULUS picks up the paper.*

ELIJAH McCOY
> Is it not enough to know that…

> *REMUS rushes towards ELIJAH. ROMULUS holds REMUS back.*

REMUS
> No, it is not!!! It is not enough!!!!! It is not…

ROMULUS
> Elijah, listen. I understand… I mean, if I were you, gosh, I'd be shouting from the highest… uhm… what we were thinking is that we wouldn't lie about it. Just if someone comes in here, we don't mention it. That's all.

ELIJAH McCOY
> And if someone asks?

ROMULUS
> Then we lie.

ELIJAH McCOY
> Has it ever occurred to you, that all the evils in this country, the hatred, and ignorance, bitterness and greed are inefficiencies that corrode the gears of our society, and

if not for this, we could truly be the greatest nation the earth has ever seen.

ROMULUS
Elijah.

ELIJAH McCOY
Gentlemen, you are more than welcome to do as you like.

ROMULUS
Now, just wait a moment.

ELIJAH McCOY
If you will excuse me, I have been asked to speak to a youth organization in Detroit, I will be there for two days. I am not going to telegraph you the name of the hotel I'm staying at because there will be no need for you to contact me again. Good afternoon.

> *ELIJAH leaves.*

ROMULUS
We still have the Buxton Manufacturing contract and the…

REMUS
Get your hand off my shoulder.

> *REMUS rubs his eyes. Blinks.*

ROMULUS
Listen, I don't know what's going on between you and Martha, but if you're sick of hotel food, and need a place to dine tonight…

REMUS
What does it mean when the vision on the edges of your sight becomes hazy.

ROMULUS
It means you see a doctor.

> *ROMULUS exits. MARY enters.*

REMUS
I suppose it does.

Actors #2, #3 and #4 enter as skaters on a rink. REMUS walks through them as if in a dream.

MARY ELEANORA DELANEY
Yooohoo! Elijah! Over here.

REMUS
I suppose it does.

REMUS exits.

ELIJAH McCOY
Mary?

MARY ELEANORA DELANEY
Tell me, Mr. McCoy, did you ever think that in the midst of a city such as this, you could find a place to put on a pair of ice skates and llllll, oops, I almost lost my…

ELIJAH McCOY
Are you alright.

MARY ELEANORA DELANEY
Oh, of course. I'll have you know I've enjoyed many a mid winter afternoon at this very rink since childhood. Comes as natural to me as… well riding a hooohoooohoooooo…

ELIJAH McCOY
I have you.

MARY ELEANORA DELANEY
Why, thank you, Mr. McCoy.

ELIJAH McCOY
I should thank you for the magnificent opportunity you provided this afternoon.

ELIJAH holds MARY's arms. She waddles in a circle.

MARY ELEANORA DELANEY
I believe you and I are much alike in our desire to see young men and women take pride in themselves and take control of their… could we sit for a moment. I'm certain your legs must be quite tired from everything you've—oh, my!

ELIJAH McCOY

Hold onto my arm, come, slowly.

She wiggles her bum in an attempt to stay balanced.

MARY ELEANORA DELANEY

Not too fast…

ELIJAH McCOY

This way. Now sit.

MARY ELEANORA DELANEY

I suppose this doesn't compare with what you were used to as a child up north.

He takes off his skates.

ELIJAH McCOY

Oh, it compares just fine. As a matter of fact I have been entertaining the idea of relocating to another city and…

MARY ELEANORA DELANEY

Really! I mean… That would be… to have someone of your calibre, of your genius, here in the community…

ELIJAH McCOY

Please, do not debase the value of such an extraordinary word.

MARY ELEANORA DELANEY

Mr. McCoy, if there is one thing Mary Eleanora Delaney despises, it is the vacuous adulation of those who rush to be kind. Any praise from my lips is heavily considered and offered with utmost sincerity.

He starts to take her skates off.

MARY ELEANORA DELANEY

Oh, you don't need to…

ELIJAH McCOY

Sometimes, if a skate is fastened too tight, it can impede circulation.

MARY ELEANORA DELANEY
> That's alright, leave it, I'm… ooooooh, thank you, soooo much. The other one. Here.

ELIJAH McCOY
> Miss Delaney.

MARY ELEANORA DELANEY
> Mr. McCoy.

ELIJAH McCOY
> I believe I would like you to accompany me to dinner tomorrow night.

> *She pulls away.*

ELIJAH McCOY
> Is something wrong?

MARY ELEANORA DELANEY
> I certainly hope you do not mistake my vociferous appreciation for your work as any indication that I am a woman of questionable moral fibre.

ELIJAH McCOY
> I simply…

MARY ELEANORA DELANEY
> Make no mistake, Mr. McCoy, I care as much for my reputation as one can care about something that once lost is impossible to regain.

ELIJAH McCOY
> Of course. Please, accept my apology. I can easily dine alone.

MARY ELEANORA DELANEY
> No, no don't do that! We can eat together. I… wanted you to know that I'm… I just wanted you to know. That's all.

> *Beat. MARY kisses ELIJAH on the lips passionately. She tries to make a dignified exit but her skates are now unlaced and she struggles to stand up. She eventually gains her composure. Nods to ELIJAH and leaves. GERTRUDE KEITH enters the stage with a shawl and a basket full of her groceries.*

GERTRUDE KEITH
Excuse me, is this the McCoy residence?

ELIJAH McCOY
Gertrude?

GERTRUDE KEITH
Hold this please.

GERTRUDE hands him the basket.

ELIJAH McCOY
Ehm…

GERTRUDE KEITH
Could you tell Mr. McCoy, I apologize for being a tad early.

ELIJAH McCOY
Gertrude…

GERTRUDE KEITH
I ain't usually in this end of town but I had to pick up a prescription for my mamma and…

ELIJAH McCOY
Miss Keith, I am Mr. McCoy.

GERTRUDE KEITH
Oh. Okay.

ELIJAH McCOY
May I take your shawl?

GERTRUDE KEITH
Thank you kindly.

ELIJAH McCOY
Come this way.

GERTRUDE KEITH
This is your house?

ELIJAH McCOY
Yes. Yes it is.

GERTRUDE KEITH
Alright.

ELIJAH McCOY

Now as the service has probably explained to you, I've just moved here from out of town, and I have found it difficult to tend to household chores and deal with my business concerns at the same time.

GERTRUDE KEITH

Alright.

ELIJAH McCOY

Initially I'm only looking for two or three days a week. Daytime only. I anticipate that as I gain more contract work, I will require a more comprehensive commitment. Is that acceptable?

GERTRUDE KEITH

Yeah. Sure.

ELIJAH McCOY

Have you… do you have any questions?

GERTRUDE KEITH

Okay. Two things: first, I will not stand being kicked, hit, bitten, or struck with any object of any kind. I take it from White folks cause I has to, but last time a Negro did that to me, I walked out da house.

ELIJAH McCOY

Oh, I would never…

GERTRUDE KEITH

Two. Keep your hands to yourself, you understand me? I got kids. I got two kids. I ain't looking for no mo. You don't like it, you don't hire me. Plain as that.

ELIJAH McCOY

Oh, I can assure you, Miss Keith, there is a woman… you will meet her. She and I… our souls are intertwined.

GERTRUDE KEITH

Your souls are "innatwined"? Oh, pardon me, I forgot, a man would never put his hands on another woman when they "souls is innatwined." How bout this, you cross the line, Imo tell her. We'll see how long your souls stay "innatwined."

ELIJAH likes her.

ELIJAH McCOY
Fair enough. Fair enough.

GERTRUDE KEITH
Monday mornin too soon?

ELIJAH McCOY
Monday morning is just fine.

GERTRUDE grabs her bag and her coat.

GERTRUDE KEITH
Then Mr. McCoy, you got yoself a maid.

She shakes his hand and leaves. DON enters the stage.

DON BOGIE
Well if it ain't the devil hiself, looking to see who's talking up his name.

ELIJAH McCOY
Donbogie.

DON BOGIE
Oh, would you look at yourself! Is that one o them horseless carriages parked right out front there easy as you please?

ELIJAH McCOY
It's... I just...

DON BOGIE
Don't just stand outside in the cold, getcha ass in here, so I can close the door.

ELIJAH McCOY
You look...

DON BOGIE
Oh, this old thang, I just wear this around here cause... you know... mighty fine when I first got it out the store though. Damn, I was a sight for sore eyes I can tell you that. Remember?

ELIJAH McCOY
Of course. Yeah.

DON BOGIE

Y'all have got to setchaself down and tell me what y'all been up to.

ELIJAH McCOY

Well, I've...

DON BOGIE

You know what y'all can do for me? Y'all have got to talk to the boys up in the head office. This is something y'all missed cuz you been away and all, but they seem to have it in they head that I was responsible for a shipment of goods that went missing. Now, I've tried to reason with those boys, but I know they gonna listen to you, you tha man, you tha real deal.

ELIJAH McCOY

Have you been drinking?

DON BOGIE

Oh, that? That's not from today. That's from last night. I tied one on, know what I'm saying? Listen, I really need you to do this for me and if you happen to have a couple hundred dollars you could lend me till the end of next week...

ELIJAH McCOY

A couple hundred dollars?

DON BOGIE

Just till the end of next week, and I know you know I'm good for it. Just to tie me over till this whole misunderstanding is worked out. It's all gonna work out. I'll be fine.

ELIJAH McCOY

Don I... I've come to say goodbye.

DON BOGIE

I beg your pardon?

ELIJAH McCOY

I've moved to Detroit.

DON BOGIE

You what?

ELIJAH McCOY

I'm getting married. I'm not coming back.

DON BOGIE

The hell does that mean?

ELIJAH McCOY

I came to say goodbye.

DON BOGIE

Step ovah here now and answer me one question. Who got you in the door, when you had no one to believe in you.

ELIJAH McCOY

Don...

DON BOGIE

Answer me this. Have I ever asked you for money before? No! Did you ever offer me any kind of support for helping you out? No.

ELIJAH McCOY

I want to be able to help you but...

He starts to shiver.

DON BOGIE

You think you would be standing here, in them fine clothes if it wasn't for me? You don't know nothing about this world until you know me. You one of those damn people always lookin at the belly side of life when the sun's shining on your face! Now I ain't funnin with ya. I ain't asking for all that you rightfully owe me. Just enough to help me get by.

ELIJAH McCOY

Well, this is... I can... here.

DON BOGIE

Three dollahs? Negro, please!

ELIJAH McCOY

That's all I can afford.

DON BOGIE

Let me see your wallet.

ELIJAH McCOY
Well Don, I... I don't really have any form of employment right now, I'm struggling just to...

DON pulls out a gun.

DON BOGIE
Let me see ya damn wallet. Elijah, I swear to God, don't make me do something I don't want to do. I am at the edge of everything. Let me see your wallet.

ELIJAH walks over to DON. Puts his hand on the gun. Hugs him.

ELIJAH McCOY
Are you cold?

DON BOGIE
I got this leak in the roof, when it rains I get this chill right to my bones.

ELIJAH McCOY
I don't know if you're gonna listen to me, but you need to understand, I really want to help you, but I can't.

ELIJAH sits DON down.

Even at this point, when all your misfortunes keep you alive for the sole purpose of observing you yearn for your own demise, you can rise up, free yourself from enslavement.

ELIJAH takes the gun out of DON's hand and places it behind them.

Search for the most efficient way to live. Make your survival a science. In the midst of our deepest sorrow, there is the comfort of knowing our lives can only get better.

MARY enters.

MARY ELEANORA DELANEY
Elijah?

ELIJAH McCOY
I have to go.

DON BOGIE
Can't you just stay for a…

ELIJAH McCOY
I have to go.

DON BOGIE
But…

ELIJAH McCOY
Don…

DON BOGIE
I understand. I understand.

DON Exits. ELIJAH walks behind MARY.

MARY ELEANORA DELANEY
Elijah McCoy, where in heaven's name are… oh, my goodness… don't lurk darling, you gave me a fright.

ELIJAH McCOY
I apologize profusely, my love, how can I help you.

MARY ELEANORA DELANEY
I do not wish to have another argument about Gertrude…

ELIJAH McCOY
My darling, we simply do not have the means to…

MARY ELEANORA DELANEY
Did I not just say…

ELIJAH McCOY
…employ her on a full time basis.

MARY ELEANORA DELANEY
Oh, good Lord, Elijah, I'm not an idiot. I understand the…

ELIJAH McCOY
Our savings are such that…

MARY ELEANORA DELANEY
I really do wish you would allow me to finish a sentence.

ELIJAH McCOY
I simply…

MARY ELEANORA DELANEY

> I need the study on the second floor available for my meeting of the Twentieth Century Club. Gertrude needs the room to finish her ironing.

ELIJAH McCOY

> Tell her to use the pantry.

MARY ELEANORA DELANEY

> My love, the board with which to iron our clothes is built into the wall. It is not intended to be moved.

> > *ELIJAH takes up paper and pencil. Starts to draw. Actor #6 enters with an ironing board. Places it behind MARY.*

> I understand our financial situation. I am not asking you to…

ELIJAH McCOY

> There.

> > *ELIJAH taps his pencil on the pad of paper. MARY turns to see the ironing board.*

MARY ELEANORA DELANEY

> What's this?

ELIJAH McCOY

> A portable ironing board with my own patented design. Adjustable height, and a tapered end for shirt collars and sleeves.

MARY ELEANORA DELANEY

> How would you…

ELIJAH McCOY

> It folds when you pull at this. It can fit neatly under one arm. You can place it in any room in the house.

MARY ELEANORA DELANEY

> Why, thank you… honey. That will do nicely.

ELIJAH McCOY

> It is my pleasure.

MARY ELEANORA DELANEY
Oh, and before I forget, if you get a chance, could you water the front lawn.

ELIJAH McCOY
Water the front lawn.

> *He starts to draw again. Actor #6 brings out a lawn sprinkler. Places it behind MARY.*

MARY ELEANORA DELANEY
I know you hate doing it, but it is essential, particularly in these summer months to…

> *ELIJAH taps his pencil on the pad of paper. MARY turns to see…*

What's this?

ELIJAH McCOY
Automatic lawn sprinkler with my own patented turtle design.

MARY ELEANORA DELANEY
Oh, how wonder…

ELIJAH McCOY
You attach the hose here. The water moves through careful application of centrifugal force.

MARY ELEANORA DELANEY
But if you're not there to observe the…

ELIJAH McCOY
I suppose one would have to move the device once or twice every ten, fifteen minutes.

MARY ELEANORA DELANEY
How would you prevent the front walk from becoming wet?

ELIJAH McCOY
What would it matter.

MARY ELEANORA DELANEY
The stones would become slippery…

He starts to draw again. Actor #6 brings out a pair of shoes.

...if I were to step too quickly, I could loose my footing. If we were to have guests...

ELIJAH taps pencil, MARY turns.

ELIJAH McCOY
A rubber soled shoe with grooves similar to those I designed for lubricating locomotives.

MARY ELEANORA DELANEY
Of course.

ELIJAH McCOY
With this design I can assure you that it would be near impossible to loose your footing in the midst of a rainstorm.

MR. BURGESS arrives at the door, knocks.

Door knocker... hmmm.

MARY takes his pencil.

MARY ELEANORA DELANEY
Stop! Just, stay. Let me get the door.

MR. BURGESS
Mary.

MARY ELEANORA DELANEY
Mr. Burgess, what a surprise.

MR. BURGESS
Yes. Uhm, I have this as the address of a Mr. McCoy.

MARY ELEANORA DELANEY
I will tell my husband that you're...

ELIJAH McCOY
Can I help you?

MR. BURGESS
Mr. McCoy, I'm not sure if you remember me, I work for the Detroit Lubricator Company.

MARY takes the ironing board, sprinkler and shoes and leaves.

ELIJAH McCOY

I remember you very well.

MR. BURGESS

Sir, there has been a sudden change in ownership and I am in desperate need of your services.

ELIJAH McCOY

Come in. Come in.

MR. BURGESS notices MARY, who wants to explain, but can't. She exits.

MR. BURGESS

Yes. Eh… thank you. Mr. McCoy, as you know, a new generation of steam engine thermodynamics is upon us. May I?

ELIJAH McCOY

By all means.

MR. BURGESS sits.

MR. BURGESS

Superheater engines, they're four times larger than their predecessor…

ELIJAH McCOY

James J. Hill at Great Northern. His design.

MR. BURGESS

Yes. Exactly. Yes. Sir, the super heated steam is too powerful, the high temperature and pressure make it too corrosive. We need a solution and we need one fast. I am more than willing to hire you on as a consultant. Any assistance, any insight you can foster would greatly be appreciated.

ELIJAH McCOY

Four times as large.

MR. BURGESS

I have all of the specifications right here.

He hands ELIJAH specifications.

ELIJAH McCOY

Then I suppose I should get to work.

He hands ELIJAH a contract.

MR. BURGESS

Here's a contract. Of course any patent rights remain in your possession. We're looking at a standard license fee…

ELIJAH McCOY

Oh, and… well, I understand that, well… if you find it necessary to, perhaps, suppress the fact that a Negro developed the device…

MR. BURGESS

Oh, that's… certainly that is something we have to… be careful about, yes, however, Mr. McCoy… I mean, for heaven's sake, it's 1913. We have finally entered a truly modern age. I certainly hope all this foolishness will soon be over with.

ELIJAH McCOY

Mr. Burgess, please call me Elijah.

MR. BURGESS puts out his hand.

MR. BURGESS

Pat.

ELIJAH McCOY

Well, Pat, enough lollygagging. My inventions have yet to invent themselves.

MR. BURGESS

Wonderful doing business with you.

He leaves. ELIJAH grabs his paper and pencil. He sharpens his pencil. He is concerned about what is to come.

ELIJAH McCOY

Superheater.

A projection of the superheater.

Modifications here and here…

LONG ISLAND JOE
These elements here convert any and all extraneous drops of water back into the system here.

ELIJAH McCOY
That must increase steam volume by…

BOSTON PETE enters.

BOSTON PETE
Efficiency increased by 35%.

ELIJAH McCOY
Beautiful.

BOSTON PETE
We have tried everything.

ELIJAH McCOY
Absolutely sublime.

LONG ISLAND JOE
We tried using more lubricating cups. We tried bigger, we tried…

BOSTON PETE
We even tried shootin the oil in through the system faster, slower…

ELIJAH McCOY
Yes. Well…

LONG ISLAND JOE
It's too powerful. The steam. It's as if the damn thing…

BOSTON PETE
It's like a vendetta.

LONG ISLAND JOE
Yeah, like the steam is trying to obliterate everything.

BOSTON PETE
Yeah.

LONG ISLAND JOE
Tear the whole thing apart.

> *LONG ISLAND JOE and BOSTON PETE exit.*
> *GERTRUDE enters.*

GERTRUDE KEITH
Mr. McCoy. Mr. McCoy?

ELIJAH McCOY
Yes.

GERTRUDE KEITH
Your tea, Mr. McCoy.

ELIJAH McCOY
Did I not inform you and my wife that I was not to be disturbed.

GERTRUDE KEITH
You ain't had no breakfast, you ain't had no lunch…

ELIJAH McCOY
Did I not tell you and my wife that I did not want to be disturbed!

GERTRUDE KEITH
Listen here…

ELIJAH McCOY
I don't need sandwiches, I don't need tea, I don't need a sweater, I don't need a goddamned thing other than to be left alone!!!

GERTRUDE KEITH
Tell you what. You got your wish!

> *GERTRUDE turns and leaves. YOUNG ELIJAH enters*
> *the stage. ELIJAH looks at his pad of paper.*

YOUNG ELIJAH McCOY
Okay, it was Papin who said air exerts pressure, so therefore a vacuum can do work.

ELIJAH McCOY
The steam is too corrosive. Hmmmm.

He sketches. Each sketch he tears up and tosses to the ground. YOUNG ELIJAH reads the paper and becomes angrier and angrier.

YOUNG ELIJAH McCOY
The efficiency of an engine is due to the temperature difference within the engine, and not the substance, such as steam, that drives the mechanism.

ELIJAH McCOY
I could… well I suppose I could change the substance from water steam to a kind of… gas perhaps.

YOUNG ELIJAH McCOY
Air exerts pressure. A vacuum can do work… I can't see.

He sketches.

ELIJAH McCOY
John Newlands is working on something, the periodicity of elements.

YOUNG ELIJAH McCOY
I can't see.

ELIJAH McCOY
The atomic weight of all substances arrange themselves into octaves. If I found…

YOUNG ELIJAH McCOY
Oh, God. I… I can't see! I CAN'T SEE!

YOUNG ELIJAH sits.

ELIJAH McCOY
Quiet! Well, let's approach it from another direction. Simplicity. I could increase the points of saturation.

BOSTON PETE and LONG ISLAND JOE enter.

BOSTON PETE
Yeah, we implemented the change you requested and it seemed to work for a period of time, however…

ELIJAH McCOY
> Not a problem, not a problem. What if we were to adjust the insertion points.

LONG ISLAND JOE
> That makes no difference. You should know that.

ELIJAH McCOY
> If... if we...

BOSTON PETE
> No.

ELIJAH McCOY
> Or...

LONG ISLAND JOE
> No.

ELIJAH McCOY
> Or...

BOSTON PETE
> Nope.

ELIJAH McCOY
> Or...

LONG ISLAND JOE
> No.

ELIJAH McCOY
> Do you mean to tell me that you have implemented everything that I have suggested to you, in the exact manner that I have instructed, and NOTHING worked?!

BOSTON PETE
> Mr. McCoy, We do not have limitless resources. Perhaps you should find your answer, then come back and talk to us.

> > *BOSTON PETE and LONG ISLAND JOE exit. ELIJAH thinks for a moment, then writes.*

ELIJAH McCOY
> *Dear William Rankine. First I must apologize profusely for not writing to you for many many years. It is I, Elijah. Recently I have*

been faced with a new challenge and I was hoping to employ your great wisdom and expertise in…

> *In the middle of ELIJAH's line, WILLIAM enters and stands facing the audience. NURSE CUGNOT enters with a blanket. She puts it on WILLIAM and he becomes old.*

NURSE CUGNOT
Dear Monsieur McCoy. My name is Charlotte Cugnot. I am responding for Mr. Rankine who got your letter after being redirected here to Canniesburn Hospital. Unfortunately Mr. Rankine has had a cardiac episode and is no longer able to speak.

> *ELIJAH closes the letter.*

YOUNG ELIJAH McCOY
I can't do it. It's too hard.

NURSE CUGNOT
I read your letter out loud to him and I could tell by the way his eyes lit up that he thought very highly of you.

YOUNG ELIJAH McCOY
I mean, maybe there are just some problems that can't be solved.

NURSE CUGNOT
For some reason, he spends many a night, staring out at the moon from his balcony for hours on end…

> *NURSE GOGNOT and WILLIAM exit. ELIJAH crumples up the letter. GEORGE enters.*

YOUNG ELIJAH McCOY
There must be a limit to what we human beings can know. Right?

> *GEORGE speaks into one of ELIJAH's ears.*

GEORGE McCOY
There is one perfect thing in this world…

YOUNG ELIJAH McCOY
Don't feel bad. There's no reason to.

GEORGE speaks into ELIJAH's other ear.

GEORGE McCOY
… and that is the will of God.

GEORGE exits.

YOUNG ELIJAH McCOY
You're not giving up. You're just accepting the way of the universe. The problem will get solved, just not by you.

ELIJAH McCOY
I don't care if… this isn't about me.

YOUNG ELIJAH McCOY
Of course not.

ELIJAH McCOY
However, it would be advantageous to our people if…

YOUNG ELIJAH McCOY
Negroes don't need or want your inventions, science, or higher learning. They love their blessed ignorance. Let them be.

ELIJAH McCOY
How dare you!

YOUNG ELIJAH McCOY
A good scientist looks at the world with a harsh, objective eye. Let go of your pride and your ego, then look me in the eye and tell me that you really believe anything you say or do can change the way people treat each other in this world.

ELIJAH McCOY
By setting an example, I can…

YOUNG ELIJAH McCOY
Nobody knows you exist. Please. Please.

YOUNG ELIJAH exits slowly. ELIJAH pulls out his pencil. Starts to write.

ELIJAH McCOY
Dear Mr. Burgess. Pat. It's me. Elijah. I… there is no easy way to

*put this. First I must thank you for your illimitable belief in me.
I understand the amount of money and resources you have...*

>   *GERTRUDE enters with her coat. MARY enters with
>   a coffee cup.*

MARY ELEANORA DELANEY
Get back here when I'm
talking to you! I can't tell
you how absolutely rude
I find your behaviour
sometimes!

GERTRUDE KEITH
Listen, if I am this much
trouble to you, I may as
well do the noble thing
and quit! Y'all can see the
back of my Black ass!

ELIJAH McCOY
Ladies!

GERTRUDE KEITH
Mr. McCoy...

MARY ELEANORA DELANEY
My darling, I have told this person time after time after time
how to properly prepare coffee for percolation!

ELIJAH McCOY
Ladies, this is not the time! Both of you, I...

GERTRUDE KEITH
Listen, y'all can make it yo damn self from now on!

>   *GERTRUDE goes to leave.*

ELIJAH McCOY
Both of you. Stop it! Now! What's the matter?

MARY ELEANORA DELANEY
Darling, you know my stomach has been extremely delicate
lately, I can hardly keep anything down, I need...

GERTRUDE KEITH
The way I make the damn coffee is the exact same way
I have always made the damn coffee...

>   *ELIJAH takes the coffee cup from MARY.*

MARY ELEANORA DELANEY
How does that explain the distinct metallic taste I have had on my tongue all morning!

GERTRUDE KEITH
Metallic what?

ELIJAH McCOY
If the two of you could…

MARY ELEANORA DELANEY
The moment I took one sip of your coffee this morning, I had a sharp metallic taste on the tip of my tongue that has lasted all day. Now…

GERTRUDE KEITH
Hold on, hold on, hold on to everything! Tell me something. Are there any foods that you suddenly start wanting to eat stronger than you've ever wanted before.

MARY ELEANORA DELANEY
Sardines and milk. Why.

GERTRUDE KEITH
Elijah, say hello to the damn mother of yo damn child.

ELIJAH McCOY	**MARY ELEANORA DELANEY**
What?	I beg your pardon?

GERTRUDE KEITH
Now, because this is your first, I ain't gonna quit just yet. The first twenty months, they's a killer. Y'all are gonna need me. Soon as that child can go to the bathroom for itself, I swear to you, I am gone. Now, if you'll scuse me, I'll get to makin dinner.

>   *GERTRUDE walks away.*

ELIJAH McCOY
But…

>   *GERTRUDE points at him to shut up, and exits.*

MARY ELEANORA DELANEY
A child?

ELIJAH McCOY
Well.

MARY ELEANORA DELANEY
Is that alright?

ELIJAH McCOY
Alright? My love, we are about to create another living, sentient being. There is nothing more complex, no charge more noble, may I feel, oh, I suppose it's still too small. What greater challenge than to countenance a stable... coffee grinds! Wait. Wait. Of course. Yes! Coffee grinds! Of course! Yes! I need...

> *He suddenly kisses MARY. Starts looking around the room.*

I love you! I need pencil. Paper. Where did I... coffee grinds. I just had... where did I...

> *MR. BURGESS enters. Sits, picks up the coffee cup. He's looking at a piece of paper with ELIJAH's new invention. MARY pulls the pencil from behind his ear, hands it to him.*

MR. BURGESS
I'm not sure I understand. Mr. McCoy?

MARY ELEANORA DELANEY
Oh, Elijah McCoy.

MR. BURGESS
Elijah?

ELIJAH McCOY
Sorry?

MR. BURGESS
Elijah...

ELIJAH McCOY
I'm sorry, my mind was elsewhere.

MR. BURGESS
How is this different from...

ELIJAH McCOY

Oh right. Yes. What I discovered is that the problem is not the lubricating device itself but the agent of lubrication.

He brings out a bottle of oil with graphite solution from his pocket.

MR. BURGESS

What's this.

ELIJAH McCOY

Even though the pressure is higher, the temperature more intense, steam is still water and oil is still oil. If the water becomes more powerful, so should the lubricating solution.

MR. BURGESS

It's so dark.

ELIJAH McCOY

Regular lubricating oil mixed with shavings of graphite. A form of carbon. Atomic weight 12.0107. The more graphite you add the stronger the solution, much like the more grounds of coffee left in a cup the stronger the blend.

ELIJAH pours coffee into MR. BURGESS's cup.

MR. BURGESS

Won't this clog up the…

ELIJAH McCOY

I've made all the necessary modifications and I have a working model up and running.

MR. BURGESS

It's so simple.

ELIJAH McCOY

That's my specialty.

MR. BURGESS

I knew it! I knew you'd be able to… oh, I could kiss you! I won't but… ah yes. Money.

MR. BURGESS writes a cheque.

MR. BURGESS
I never had any doubt in my mind whatsoever! This is truly you're finest...

ELIJAH McCOY
Did you make that out to McCoy...

MR. BURGESS
Manufacturing. Of course I did. I certainly hope this is the beginning of many more fruitful business interactions.

ELIJAH McCOY
That is my hope as well.

MR. BURGESS
Elijah, my wife and I would love for you to stop by the house sometime, she's French and loves a good confit of duck but she would never waste such fine cuisine on just little old me...

ELIJAH McCOY
Name the time and the place.

MR. BURGESS
Wonderful doing business with you. Absolutely wonderful.

> *MR. BURGESS exits, MARY enters.*

MARY ELEANORA DELANEY
I told you he would love it.

ELIJAH McCOY
It's odd isn't it. I was so nervous going in and...

MARY ELEANORA DELANEY
Oh, you just love being a mystery, that's all.

> *ELIJAH starts the car.*

ELIJAH McCOY
Well, I thought that I would first take us to the bank and deposit the first payment to McCoy Manufacturing...

MARY ELEANORA DELANEY
And then to a restaurant of my choosing.

ELIJAH McCOY
Which reminds me, Mr. Burgess has invited us to his place one evening for dinner and I accepted.

MARY ELEANORA DELANEY
You told him I was pregnant?

Actors #5 and #6 walk onstage with the broom and mop. They turn them upside down.

ELIJAH McCOY
Well, no but…

MARY ELEANORA DELANEY
Darling…

ELIJAH McCOY
I can tell him tomorrow…

MARY ELEANORA DELANEY
It's something they should know, that's all.

ELIJAH McCOY
Yes I supp…

Actors #5 and #6 slam the handles on the stage. Time stops. Car accident. All the other actors enter the stage. Actor #3 plays a high note on the harmonica. Actors #5 and #6 sing the same note. Two beats later Actor #6 brings his note down a semi-tone. Actors #2 and #4 take the cheque and hat from MARY. Once this is done, all of the actors except MARY and ELIJAH, repeat words from the CHORUS line below. MARY and ELIJAH stand, tumble forward. MARY is handed the bowl of water from Actor #3. She puts her hands in the water and puts the water on her face. She takes the bowl off stage. ELIJAH sits and Actor #3 becomes DR. TILLY.

CHORUS
Fire. Water. Piston. Train. Car. Steam. White. Back. Forth. Help. Can't. Hear. You. I.

DR. TILLY
I said can you hear me?

ELIJAH McCOY

Yes, I can now. Yes.

DR. TILLY

As I have said, you may experience some sharp discomfort in your left hip, or your right ankle. I am writing you a prescription for a painkiller, you take one, then an hour later, you take another. Never exceed 8 within a 24-hour period.

ELIJAH McCOY

Thank you. Dr….

DR. TILLY

Tilly. Dr. Tilly.

> As *ELIJAH stands and looks around for MARY, he limps due to his injuries.*

ELIJAH McCOY

Oh. Wait. Mary! Oh, my goodness! Where is she? Oh, my goodness!!!! Is she alright?

DR. TILLY

Mr. McCoy…

ELIJAH McCOY

Can I see her? Is she okay? Is she hurt? Is it bad? Answer me! Answer me!!!!

DR. TILLY

Your wife and child are dead.

ELIJAH McCOY

My first wife. Anne Elizabeth.

DR. TILLY

Mary Eleanora Delaney. And your child. They are both dead.

ELIJAH McCOY

Oh. I see. I see.

DR. TILLY

We talked about this yesterday, remember?

ELIJAH McCOY
Yes. Of course. Yes. I remember. Yes.

DR. TILLY
Mr. McCoy, you're free to go.

ELIJAH McCOY
Thank you sir. Thank you.

DR. TILLY
I'm truly sorry.

ELIJAH McCOY
Yes. Thank you. Thank you.

> *DR. TILLY exits. ELIJAH limps offstage. MR.*
> *BURGESS and MR. LESSING enter.*

MR. BURGESS
Mr. Lessing, I can absolutely understand why Bolton
Industries would be intrigued by the McCoy Superheater
Lubricating Device.

MR. LESSING
I must admit I find it hard to believe that this device will do
as you say.

MR. BURGESS
We have already tested it with… now watch your step. Oh,
would you look at that.

MR. LESSING
What is this?

MR. BURGESS
It looks like one of those water sprinklers.

MR. LESSING
Interesting.

MR. BURGESS
Elijah. Elijah? I have someone here I would like you to meet.
Elijah?

> *ELIJAH enters. He is unkempt.*

ELIJAH McCOY
Yes. What. Yesssss. Yes yes yes. What?

MR. BURGESS
Oh. We can come back later.

ELIJAH McCOY
Please, come in. Wait. Who is this.

MR. BURGESS
Uhm, Elijah, this is Mr. Lessing, he owns a manufacturing company…

ELIJAH McCOY
Get in. Now! Move. Yes. Right.

MR. BURGESS takes ELIJAH inside.

MR. BURGESS
Elijah, are you alright?

ELIJAH McCOY
He's from a manufacturing company and wants to see me, eh?

MR. BURGESS
Elijah…

ELIJAH McCOY
How did you find out. Hmmm?

MR. BURGESS
About…

ELIJAH McCOY
Fascinating. Fascinating but I'm not amused. You're here obviously to see the new device I'm working on.

MR. BURGESS
New device?

ELIJAH McCOY
Please. Well, of course. I understand. A device of this magnitude, well… it will revolutionize the very fabric of the way we perceive the nature of the universe.

MR. BURGESS
What device is this?

ELIJAH McCOY
A machine that will allow a man to travel to the moon, and back.

MR. BURGESS
Oh. Elijah…

ELIJAH McCOY
Getting a man to the face of the moon poses it's own challenges, but to get that same man back!!!!? Why that, that is a slap in the face to the almighty himself.

MR. BURGESS
Uhm…

ELIJAH McCOY
Socrates spoke of the afterlife in a way that alluded to shafts that transferred souls from here to the netherworld. My plan, a massive iron shaft, that would use steam to shoot a passenger inside a massive steel bullet. Leonardo Da Vinci's Architonnerre. You follow?

MR. BURGESS
Yes. Sure.

MR. BURGESS exits during the speech.

ELIJAH McCOY
That face. I understand. You are a man of science, as am I. But you cannot turn a blind eye to passion, the soul, whimsy, dreams. The universe is an intelligible whole, a teleological whisper, just barely audible to those with hearts to see and eyes to mold the shape of our destiny. The right hand of God. The left hand of God are nothing to me now. I am light. I am the bluest flame. Come hold my hand. You see how cold? Mary? Could you get… harrrrrrghghghghg gggrrruh… oh, yes. Right. No! My eyes. They're burning!!! My EYES!!!! I can see. I can see the universe, the order of all things, it's all so simple. So beautiful. It is all so plain to me now.

DR. RABB walks up to ELIJAH.

DR. RABB
Your name sir?

ELIJAH McCOY
Where am I?

DR. RABB
You are in a hospital. Your name sir?

ELIJAH McCOY
McCoy. Elijah McCoy. Inventor of the McCoy lubricating cup.

He coughs.

DR. RABB
You believe you invented a lubricating cup.

ELIJAH McCOY
I don't believe, I know. I am Elijah McCoy. I invented the McCoy self-lubricating cup. I'm sure you've heard of it.

DR. RABB
Very good. Nurse, could I see you for a second.

NURSE BLODGETT
Doctor?

DR. RABB
Delusional. Possible violent tendencies. Call Eliose Infirmary, have them pick him up.

NURSE BLODGETT
Yes, Doctor. Come right this way, Mr. McCoy.

She leads ELIJAH to a bed.

ELIJAH McCOY
What are you doing.

NURSE BLODGETT
We're going to take very good care of you.

ELIJAH McCOY
What are you doing? I shouldn't be here, I am a graduate of

Edinburgh University! I should be treated with greater respect than this!

> *The nurse laughs.*

Madam, I am not making a joke. I am Elijah McCoy! Master engineer! Inventor of the McCoy self-lubricating cup!

> *He resists her, she twists his thumb, he succumbs.*

NURSE BLODGETT
That must have been very hard to do.

ELIJAH McCOY
I invented the McCoy lubricating cup. I revolutionized the steam engine!

NURSE BLODGETT
I'll be right back.

> *The nurse leaves. ELIJAH coughs.*

ELIJAH McCOY
But I… where are you going. I am telling you, I am Elijah McCoy! I was born in Colchester, Upper Canada. My father's house… common area… my room, a converted storage room… *(cough)* A thin cloth, hung over a… a… *(cough)* Come back…. Nurse…. I don't feel so…

> *He vomits.*

Nurse. Nurse, I think there's something wrong with me. I… *(cough)* I'm not feeling so well, and I… I think I'm going to be sick again, and I…

> *He throws up violently. There's blood in his vomit.*

Nurse! Nurse! Help me. Something's wrong. There's blood, I see blood. Help me. Help me please.

> *He starts to cry.*

Why won't somebody help me. Please. Somebody PLEASE!

> *He vomits violently all over the bed. MILDRED appears with towel and water basin.*

MILDRED McCOY
Elijah? Elijah!

ELIJAH McCOY
Who's there?

MILDRED McCOY
Elijah McCoy?

ELIJAH McCOY
Who are you?

MILDRED McCOY
Oh… my Lord. I can see your father so clearly.

ELIJAH McCOY
Mother?

MILDRED McCOY
May I hold you? Please. Oh, my good Lord, PLEASE. May I hold you in my arms. Oh, my Lord! Please, may I? Please?

> *He slowly reaches out to her. She holds him. She kisses him over and over again.*

Oh, my son. Oh! I cannot tell you how much I've longed for this! Oh, my good Lord!

ELIJAH McCOY
I surrender. I surrender.

MILDRED McCOY
Shhhh shh. Oh, my baby. Oh, my baby boy. Look at you. My son. Dear, oh, dear. We're gonna have to make you whole again.

> *With one arm she holds onto him, with the other, she takes a rag out of the water basin, cleans him up.*

ELIJAH McCOY
They don't believe me, that I'm Elijah McCoy, Mom, they don't believe me.

MILDRED McCOY
I know, baby. I know.

ELIJAH McCOY
It's not fair.

MILDRED McCOY
Maybe you're not, honey pie.

ELIJAH McCOY
But…

MILDRED McCOY
Maybe you're just a whisper. A particle and a wave all at the same time.

ELIJAH McCOY
I…

> *GEORGE steps onto the stage.*

GEORGE McCOY
The world…

ELIJAH McCOY
Daddy.

> *WILLIAM steps onto the stage.*

WILLIAM RANKINE
The world is a complete harmony…

ELIJAH McCOY
William.

> *MR. BURGESS enters.*

MR. BURGESS
…whose sweetest mysteries…

ELIJAH McCOY
Mr. Burgess.

> *MARY enters.*

MARY ELEANORA DELANEY
…intimate the possibility of a life without suffering, without fear.

ELIJAH McCOY
Mary!

DON enters.

DON BOGIE
It is our responsibility to struggle to achieve our true potential.

ELIJAH McCOY
Don.

CHORUS
A full and generous love of our fellow man is within our grasp.

MR. BURGESS & WILLIAM RANKINE
I can feel it.

DON BOGIE & GEORGE McCOY
I can feel it.

MARY ELEANORA DELANEY
I can feel it.

ELIJAH McCOY
Mother, I love you so much.

ELIJAH cries. His mother holds him with all her strength and with great joy exclaims.

MILDRED McCOY
I love you too, son. I love you too.

End

Andrew Moodie

Actor, writer, director Andrew Moodie has performed in many of Canada's most distinguished theatres; Second City, Soulpepper, Alberta Theatre Projects, Prairie Theatre Exchange, Neptune Theatre, Eastern Front Theatre, the National Arts Centre, the Stratford Festival, Theatre Passe Muraille, Factory Theatre, and the Canadian Stage Company, to name a few. He garnered a Dora nomination for Best Male Performance for his portrayal of Othello for Shakespeare in the Rough's production of *Othello* and he won a Dora Award for his performance in Roseneath Theatre's *Health Class*. His television and film appearances include playing Dr. Hyde in "Side Effects" for CBC, and Rachel Crawford's evil boyfriend in Clement Virgo's feature film "Rude." His first play *Riot* was performed at the legendary Factory Theatre, where it received an extended run and won the prestigious Chalmers award for Best New Play. His other plays include: *Oui, A Common Man's Guide to Loving Women* and *The Lady Smith*. He also directed the first production of *The Real McCoy*. Other directing credits include: Michael Miller's *The Power of Harriet T!* for the Manitoba Theatre for Young People and *for coloured girls who have considered suicide/when the rainbow is enuf* for the coloUred girls' collective.